Drink

YOUR

Garden

Drink
YOUR
Garden

Recipes, Stories, and Tips from the Simple Goodness Cocktail Farm

---

BELINDA KELLY *AND*
VENISE CUNNINGHAM

PHOTOGRAPHS BY RYLEA FOEHL

Countryman Press
An Imprint of W. W. Norton & Company
Independent Publishers Since 1923

This book of drink recipes is intended as a general information resource. Please be careful not to use any ingredients to which you are allergic or that might interfere with medications you are taking. If you forage for wild flowers or other drink ingredients, please be sure that you know which kinds of flowers and other plants are safe to collect. Please pay careful attention to the directions for preserving and storing different products and only rely on reliable sources of information about canning. The commercial products that the authors recommend in this book are ones that the authors personally like. You need to do your own research to find the ones that are best for you. Any URLs displayed in this book link or refer to websites that existed as of press time. The publisher is not responsible for, and should not be deemed to endorse or recommend, any website other than its own or any app or content that it did not create. The authors, also, are not responsible for any third-party material.

Copyright © 2025 by Belinda Kelly and Venise Cunningham
Photographs © 2025 by Rylea Foehl

Printed in China

For information about permission to reproduce selections from this book, write to Permissions, Countryman Press, 500 Fifth Avenue, New York, NY 10110

For information about special discounts for bulk purchases, please contact W. W. Norton Special Sales at specialsales@wwnorton.com or 800-233-4830

Manufacturing by Toppan Leefung Pte. Ltd.
Book design by Laura Palese
Production manager: Devon Zahn

Countryman Press
www.countrymanpress.com

An imprint of W. W. Norton & Company, Inc.
500 Fifth Avenue, New York, NY 10110
www.wwnorton.com

978-1-68268-879-3

10 9 8 7 6 5 4 3 2 1

To Doris, who was Simply Good, and to our
Grandma Nanc, who is the life of every party.

CONTENTS

Introduction 11

GARDEN-TO-GLASS
DRINK MAKING 20

THE COCKTAIL
GARDEN 32

SYRUPS AND CORDIALS 46

Basic Flavored Simple Syrup 48
Strawberry Syrup 50
Blackberry and Mint Syrup 51
Spruce (or Fir) Tip Syrup 53
Lime Basil Syrup 54
Lavender Honey Syrup 57
Oleo Saccharum with Herbs 58
Citrus Cordial 59
Lilac Cordial 60
Foraged Elderflower Cordial 61
Pumpkin Spice Syrup 62
Cranberry Rosemary Syrup 65
Apple Butter 66

SHRUBS 68

Basic Shrub 70
Strawberry, Pepper, and Mint Shrub 71
Lemon Chamomile Shrub 73
Celery Shrub 74
No-Waste Spiced Lime Shrub, aka Ginger Switchel 75
Beet Shrub 77
Onyx Oxymel, or Honey Shrub 78
Fig Cardamom Shrub 80
Pepper Hot Sauce 81

TINCTURES, LIQUEURS,
AND INFUSED SPIRITS 82

Basic Liqueur 85
Herb Tincture 86
Pepper Tincture 87
Barkeep's Citrus Bitters 89
Compound Gin 90
Buzz Button Gin 92
Cherry Whiskey and Whiskey-Soaked Cherries 95
Jalapeño Tequila 96
Poblano Liqueur 99
Veggie Garden Vodka 100
Kale and Chard Vodka 101
Berry Rum and Berry Liqueur 105
Elderflower (or Lilac) Liqueur 106
Brown Butter Vodka 107
Orchardist Liqueur 107
Fennelcello 109

JUICES, TEAS,
AND DEHYDRATING 110

Fresh-Pressed Apple Cider 114
Green Juice 116
Fresh Tomato Juice 117
Botanical Waters 119
Hang-Drying Flowers and Herbs 120
Drying Flowers and Herbs for Tea 122
Floral Tea Blend (Non-Caffeinated) 125
Stone Fruit Tea 126
Sun Tea 126
Distilled Floral Water 127

7

GARNISHES 130

Fancy Ice 135

Candied Citrus Peels 136

Citrus Wheels 138

Chive Flower Braids 139

Bloody Mary Skewers 140

Herb Bouquets 141

Mojito Berries 144

Spicy Herb Garden Salt 147

Fennel Pollen Salt 148

Floral Salt or Sugar 148

Herb Sugar 149

Vanilla Sugar 149

Quick-Pickled Garlic Scapes, Asparagus,
or Green Beans 152

Pickled Carrots 153

Pickled Cucamelons 155

Quick-Pickled Garlic Dill Cucumbers 156

Pickled Celery 157

Pickled Chive Blossoms 158

NONALCOHOLIC
DRINKS 160

Strawberries and Cream Soda 163

Simple Syrup Soda 164

Shrub Soda 164

Bitters & Soda 166

Nonalcoholic Buck 167

Fresh Lemonade by the Pitcher 168

Cordial Spritz 169

Iced Tea 170

At High Noon 171

Creamy Tea Cobbler 173

Dirty Soda and the Classic Egg Cream 174

Hot Spiced Cider 175

Iced Coffee 176

COCKTAILS 178

Hard Seltzer or Ranch Water 181

Sparkling Rosé Wine Spritzer 182

Buck 183

Red Skies at Night 184

Lilac and Lead French 75 185

Making Hay Shandy 187

Old-Fashioned 188

Margarita 190

Bee's Knees 192

Roman's Empire 192

White Sangria 194

Clarified Milk Punch 197

Coastal Collins 198

Bloody Bunny 201

Garden Gibson 202

Elderflower Spritz 203

Spruce Drop 204

Crown Jewel 205

Green Goddess 206

Elderflower Vesper 206

Among the Wildflowers 208

Walk in the Woods 209

Marionberry Mojito 210

Southside 213

Smash 215

Midnight at the Movies 215

Cucumber Basil Gimlet 216

The Dashing Gentleman 218

Back Porch Lemonade 219

Pitcher Punch 221

Bloody Mary 222

Verde Maria 224

Michelada 224

Seattle Sling 227

Cock's Crow 228

Apple Betty Martini 229

8

Bonfire 229

Homecoming Margarita 231

Nancy's Whiskey Sour 232

Home for the Holidays on the Ranch (to Find Love) 235

Plenty Good 236

Pumpkin Spice Espresso Martini 237

Sparkler 239

Harvest Moon Punch 240

Hot Toddy 242

Shoalwater Sea Breeze 244

Heart Beet 245

Figgy Pudding Fizz 245

Bull's Blood & Bourbon 247

"It Was Mutual" Highball 248

Acknowledgments 249   *Index 251*

INTRODUCTION

Our Story, as Written by Belinda

Drinking from our gardens is the most joyful way we've found of pursuing self-sufficiency. My sister and I planted our first gardens a decade ago and have grown in our kitchen confidence and our harvests each year. I am a home cook and bartender who followed a winding path to launch a business, Simple Goodness Sisters, with my real-life sister Venise, who is four years older and our chief farmer. The farmer sister and the bartender sister: we wear a lot of hats in our business, but those are the two that fit us most comfortably. We make drink syrups, bitters, shrubs, ferments, and more from our farm harvests and own a bar with a garden-to-glass beverage program.

The urge to farm seems like it often skips a generation, and that's our story. We grew up in a big, close-knit family with dozens of cousins and grandparents who each had small homesteads in the Kent Valley of Washington State. Our mother, Denise, was the baby of eight kids. Her mother (our grandmother Nanny) was a fantastic cook with a prolific kitchen garden and a basement of dusty shelves with

dated Ball canning jars, filled with her harvests (the smell of those shelves will never leave me, its memory is so vivid). Our own mother didn't enjoy time in the kitchen and never grew a garden when we were growing up. She was the least enthusiastic hired berry picker of her siblings, in the days when a farm bus would pick up kids in the Kent Valley and drop them off at the fields. Her older siblings picked dutifully to earn spending money and new school clothes. She recalls hiding in the rows, waiting out the hours until she could go home. By contrast, I pick and make myself a blackberry pie with my boys every year as a birthday present to myself; that's how much I enjoy the quiet hours of plucking berries into buckets. The lessons of our grandmothers trickled down in time. It is entirely possible that it is this distance our mom gave us from the cooking and gardening life that allowed us to find our own path to it, and then to find the pursuits endlessly inspiring.

The women in our family are taught to be capable over ornamental, and for this we are very thankful. We grew up watching our Nanny and

great-aunts can all kinds of pickles and preserves, forage huckleberries in Mount Rainier National Park for jam, and bake elaborate birthday cakes with several layers and rich buttercream frostings. Making things at home was not about winning motherhood or showing off for friends, in those days; it was thrifty for a big family, and it was fun to do. Our paternal grandmother, Nancy, is a social butterfly with the hosting skills of a blue-collar Martha Stewart. Through years of raising her kids on a small farmstead in Kent, as well as livestock to keep the family meat locker full, she collected a giant tribe of 4-H friends, neighbors, fellow sports parents, church folk, and everyone in between, and she entertained them all. Her home has always been a roving happy hour of friends just stopping by at all hours for her well-stocked bar, snacks scattered around the living room in beautiful, collected-over-a-lifetime dishes, and Patsy Cline on the stereo.

Now that we have homes and families of our own, we have each embraced a home of making, doing, and growing. I am happiest in the din of a crowded kitchen, surrounded by women and their stories, and by the smells of the things they have made to help tell their stories, one bite or drink at a time. As soon as my husband, Troy, and I were married with a house of our own, I planted my first garden, complete with upside-down tomato cages (kindly pointed out to me by Great-Aunt Sylvia). Gardening is a skill like any other, and it took both Venise and me some studying and practice, but each season we got better at growing things. As soon as we began gardening, we realized why our Nanny's basement was lined with shelves, each boasting a rainbow of colorful jars with hand-labeled lids: growing is a gateway to preserving.

Growers cannot bear to throw out or waste what they've spent months carefully tending, and so they must create something, anything. The same plant that gives you a crisp and refreshing salad this month can give you a pickle, a sauce, or a cocktail syrup next winter, when the garden is frozen over. This security of a full shelf of homemade goods is one we had never known the joy of until we looked at a counter full of mason jars we'd just filled and saw a season of our lives captured within those jars, with hand-lettered lids and dates.

Our foray into preserving and growing overlapped nicely with Venise's building of her farmstead. In 2013, Venise bought a 10-acre farm. She Googled "most profitable crop to grow on small acreage" and decided on heirloom garlic, beginning her career as a farmer, while still commuting three hours daily to her day job in Seattle. She and her husband refurbished run-down barns, tilled a garden in the overgrown fields, built raised beds, raised a small herd of Nigerian dairy goats, and brought the first cows to graze in their pastures.

By 2016, with new babies on our hips, we dreamed of a livelihood away from the corporate grind, one that would allow us to spend more time with our families. My husband, Troy, transformed a 1967 Aladdin travel trailer into my dream bar on wheels and I took the leap to start a cocktail catering company. At my very first public event, Venise was helping barback and the seed was planted in her mind for what would become Simple Goodness Sisters Syrups when she heard customers ask about the unique mixers in their drinks. For the next four years, I poured drinks to help my clients toast to their biggest life events with beautifully seasonal craft cocktails. On her farm, Venise grew many of the ingredients for my menu and worked on convincing me to bottle this "secret sauce." We launched Simple Goodness Syrups in 2018 with our first three cocktail syrups: Rhubarb Vanilla Bean, Marionberry Mint, and Huckleberry Spruce Tip.

As we grew the business, we dreamed of a way to share our garden-to-glass drinks with people outside the exclusive private events I served, and within our own community. Venise found property in the small mountain town of Wilkeson, just up the road from the farm and home to 500 year-round residents. We opened a tasting room for our syrups in 2020, rebuilding a historical café, bar, and soda fountain to be a gathering place for our community.

Today, my sister and I find constant inspiration among the rows of Simple Goodness Cocktail Farm to develop new food and beverage recipes. I often throw new seed packs Venise's way as ideas spark and eagerly await the moment when, many months and much hard work later, Venise grows the seeds into an ingredient that can be mixed, infused, juiced, and ultimately bring someone joy in a delicious drink. We love to learn traditional ways of making delicious things and preserving the flavors of each season through these methods. We hope that you learn a new skill through this book, that the recipes within are used to celebrate your big and small life moments, and overall that this book gives you the confidence and inspiration to drink what you grow (or buy at a farmers' market or local shop), upside-down tomato cages or not!

Drink Your Garden: Reclaiming a Happier Hour

We've found happy hour, fresh from the garden, to be one of life's utmost simple pleasures. We're into what you might call "homesteading, light." We live an easy drive away from several grocery stores and don't have to work our land for everything we need. Instead, we choose to invest our time and energy into learning the parts of that lost art of homemaking that we genuinely love and get a lot back from, both practically and in everyday joy.

Venise has always been an animal person and loves looking out to a field full of cows, so she will always have a small herd of animals to feed her family. I stress-relief bake and have been known to bring sourdough bowls to a bonfire with friends to keep to my proofing schedule. We both keep a kitchen garden and delight in the occasional, ultrasatisfying meal made entirely from what we've grown and made.

We're into growing, preparing, and preserving our own food and drinks for the skills of it, the patience it requires of us, and the way it is, undeniably, better for our bodies. And we've found this way of drinking to be, well, life changing.

15

The Case for Slow Food and Drinks

The slow food movement celebrates the idea that food can and should be a central part of the rhythm of our daily lives. Slow food can be a revelation in abundance; it is a way of life for us, not just a menu trend. Drinking and eating local and seasonal food is a way of marking the seasons naturally, and a way to care for and nurture ourselves and our families. It trades some convenience for more connection. An understanding of the patience, hard work, and skills needed to produce food will make anyone appreciate a plate of food or a drink differently. You can absolutely do this by purchasing high-quality food grown and raised in your area by producers who put much effort and love into their work, and by taking the time to know who those folks are and what they do. Or you can dive into that work yourself, and try your own hand at it.

Growing food takes effort, dedicated attention, and lots of time spent outdoors and offline, all of which are dwindling in our current world, yet are proven necessary to our mental and physical well-being. Dirt itself is a proven antidepressant! In your first years of gardening, you may not yield a ton of every vegetable or fruit you try to grow, but a garden will reward you in other ways. And once you do get the hang of a crop and end up with your first bumper harvest, it hooks you. Not only will you learn a lot of ways to prepare zucchini or kale, and therefore probably double your vegetable intake, it becomes hard to waste, hard to abuse, and hard to overlook the importance of food in our lives when you grow and cook it yourself.

Garden to Glass

The same thoughtfulness gleaned from the farm-to-table movement is revolutionary when applied to drinks. We call this drink-making style "garden to glass." Learning to cook at home and grow your own garden changes the way you think about fast food and brings care back to the process of feeding yourself. It sounds clichéd to anyone who hasn't done it, but a person can and will get giddy about the first pea pod they get to crack open in spring. So, too, can making drinks from scratch—from ingredients you grew at home—change the way you might otherwise imbibe.

Who among us hasn't picked up a convenience pack of hard seltzers and accidentally had more than we should, without a thought about it until the dreaded hangxiety kicks in the next day? You will get giddy the first time you make a perfectly foamed sour, and we promise you, it will bring you satisfaction that you cannot buy in a can. It might even change the way you approach drinking, or how much you drink when you change your definition of what really constitutes a "happy hour," or what we prefer to call "happier hour."

17

Low-ABV and Alcohol-Free Imbibing

Happy hour is a unique opportunity for togetherness in that dear time between a full day and the evening wind-down, and it need not include alcohol. We believe that everyone deserves an invite to the party, whether they're drinking alcohol or not. Many of our family members have chosen to abstain completely from alcohol, and others have suffered from its hold on them. We always want to have something delicious to offer everyone, and we think you're going to love the nonalcoholic and low-alcohol-content options in this book. We've noted the ABV (alcohol by volume) for every recipe to help guide you.

We absolutely hope that you feel more empowered to serve something delicious to your non-alcohol-drinking friends and family. We often bring our kids into this ritual with a slowdown drink. It's a great time to catch up with them, talk about the day, and maybe finish up a few small dinner prep chores, snapping the ends off of string beans while we talk over a round.

If cocktails and zero-proof drinks line the gateway that leads you to be more curious or intentional about your food, then we've done what we set out to do. We hope that these recipes introduce you to some new ideas, new flavors, and most of all, some new friends. The best recipes aren't the ones we write with complicated ingredients and techniques; they are the ones you turn to again and again, dog-ear and spill on, and share with friends—to bring your people together. Cheers to your happier hour!

19

GARDEN-TO-GLASS

DRINK
MAKING

Tips for Using This Book

USE THE BEST INGREDIENTS YOU CAN

Use the freshest, in-season ingredients you can find. Whether they come from farmers' markets or a grocery store or your own backyard, you will be taking time and putting care into crafting each recipe, so the base ingredients should be the best they can be. The fresher the ingredient is, the more pronounced the flavors will taste.

GROW YOUR OWN

For an even deeper dive into slow food, try growing a garden—even a small container one. An herb garden can be grown indoors on a windowsill and is an excellent place to start. As reformed black thumbs, we can tell you with the authority of people who once put in their tomato cages upside down: you CAN do this.

To garden is to test your own optimism, to dare to believe in tomorrow and the harvests it can bring. You will have failures, and you will learn from them; you will have successes, and you will drink from them. Treat your garden as your grocery store, and challenge yourself each season to use what you have growing at that time in these recipes.

GET WILD

Make it your own: There are so many possible combinations of flavor that it is impossible to include all the recipes here, so please use those we provide in this book as a jumping-off point. The basic recipes are included alongside the infusion chart so as to give you the information needed to explore your own drink-making experiments. We give you full, unbridled permission to alter the basic recipes to reflect what is in season near you.

Think in layers: Don't make just a simple syrup, or a lime simple syrup, make a lime basil simple syrup! Combining multiple ingredients within each recipe creates layers of flavor. Likewise, combining multiple types of base recipes from this book within

each drink you make, such as pairing an infused vodka recipe with a syrup recipe and a garden garnish, will result in an exciting cocktail. Nothing will be more satisfying than, say, a cucumber and mint simple syrup mixed into a margarita with jalapeño pepper–infused tequila, garnished with dried chile peppers and orange rings.

FAMILY AFFAIR

Drinking is meant to be communal, so call your people. Making things is more fun with a buddy pitting cherries besides you shooting the ya know what. Don't forget to include little ones. Happier hour with your kids may seem odd within the context of American drinking culture, but in other countries, it's a normalized and intentional way to spend time with one another. With drinks in hand, you'll discuss the day's events or all their hopes and dreams. The nonalcoholic recipes in this book give you options to bring people of all ages into your cocktail (or mocktail!) hour.

WHOLE-ANIMAL BARTENDING

Just as a good hunter and butcher is taught to use all parts of an animal as a sign of respect and reverence for the food, try to use your ingredients to their fullest potential. We call this whole-animal bartending. The idea is to get the most food as possible out of the harvests you reap, with the least amount of waste. So, do a lot of things with each component. Citrus can be juiced for recipes, then the peels sliced and candied for a garnish, or the peels and pulp added to a shrub. Herbs can garnish drinks, flavor liqueurs, be hung to dry for winter teas, infuse into syrups and bitters, and be chopped fresh for a warm ricotta dip to be served for happier hour. Working this way with harvests will help you extend your garden season so you can enjoy the flavors year-round. Hang dry, dehydrate, freeze, pickle, and can fresh ingredients in season to stock your bar cart and pantry for cooler seasons when less will be growing. It's a fun challenge to reduce waste in your kitchen, and it will save you money.

Equipment and Pantry List

We don't expect you to be a trained bartender and no one will be awarding prizes for perfectly shaved ice, so this list is simple. These supplies will make the recipes easier and improve results. We encourage you to borrow or thrift some of these more specific items, like juicers, from a friend as you need them. Thrift stores are our favorite spot to find bulky kitchen appliances, such as juicers, dehydrators, and blenders because most people will donate them after using them just a few times.

Jigger: This is our only nonnegotiable tool on this list. Shot glass measurements will not be precise enough, as cocktail recipes are written down to ¼ ounce. You can use any type you like, but be sure there are interior lines to make it easy to measure. Our favorite jigger sizes are 1 ounce on one side, with interior measurements for ¼ and ½ ounce, and 1½ ounces on the other side, with an interior measurement for ¾ ounce.

Long-handled barspoon: These have long, twisted handles for smooth stirring, the spoon is used as a measurement that is less than ¼ ounce, and the twisted shaft allows you to slow the flow of liquid as you pour to create layers in a drink.

Muddler: You can buy one, or you can use the handle of a wooden spoon.

Shaker: Our top choice is a Boston shaker—this is two metal mixing tins that fit together to seal (the choice for most bar pros). A cocktail shaker with built-in strainer (called a cobbler strainer) also works, or you can even use a mason jar or wide-mouth water bottle with a tight-fitting lid.

22

GARDEN-TO-GLASS DRINK MAKING

Hawthorne strainer: This is necessary to strain out fruit pieces, pulp, and ice shards if you don't have a cobbler-style shaker with a built-in strainer.

Fine-mesh strainer and cheesecloth: This is the manual way to get a very fine strain of liqueurs and spirits. Alternatively, a CHEMEX coffee brewer with very fine, disposable paper coffee filters is a nice option to invest in and will be worthwhile to add if you will be making many of those recipes. Bonus: It also makes great drip coffee.

Paring knife and cutting board: A sharp, short blade helps cut fruit and shave off twists; the cutting board will protect your counters or bar top.

Ice cube tray: Large cubes (about 2 × 2 × 2 inches) are ideal, as they are needed for stirred, alcohol-forward drinks, such as the old-fashioned, and they can be broken into smaller chunks or crushed manually as needed.

Immersion blender or stand blender: An immersion blender is small to store and useful beyond this book for sauces, soups, etc. However, if you already have a stand blender, you can use it instead.

Baking sheets: For drying fruit and herbs.

Clean glass bottles with tight-fitting lids, such as swing-top bottles, recycled vinegar or sauce bottles, or mason jars with wide-mouth lids.

Optional: Extraction juicer, citrus press juicer, dehydrator, cherry pitter, and Y-peeler for making twists.

GLASSWARE

This book aims for simplicity wherever possible, to keep bartending a fun, part-time habit and not an expensive one. To this end, we recommend only three glass types:

Coupe: Stemmed, delicate, with a short, wide bowl, holds 5 to 7 ounces. For drinks served without ice. Excellent for Champagne and sours; the wide bowl distributes scent and the stem protects the glass from your hand warming the iceless drink.

Collins glass: Tall, straight-sided; holds about 12 ounces; great for drinks with tea, juice, club soda, tonic, etc. Fill it all the way up with ice before straining in your cocktail!

Old-fashioned or rocks glass: Heavy-bottomed, straight-sided short glass; holds 12 to 14 ounces. Suits a variety of shaken or stirred drinks served with ice.

Optional: martini glass, stemmed wineglass.

Garden-to-Glass Pantry

You'll need some ingredients you can't grow or find at a farmers' market. You can certainly add more than these, but for the sake of keeping it easy, here is what you should stock.

Cane sugar: You only need to stock one kind for most recipes: granulated cane sugar. If you'd like to experiment using different sugar types in the shrub and syrup recipes, you may. We use organic cane sugar.

Coarse sugar: For the Vanilla Sugar (page 149) and Floral Sugar (page 148) recipes. Turbinado sugar, such as Sugar In The Raw, is most readily available at your local grocery store, and will have an amber color. If you prefer your sugar rims to be white sugar, bakery supply shops online will have coarse sparkling sugar crystals. King Arthur Baking Company is a good source.

Flaky sea salt: Coarse, larger, craggy-shaped crystals perfect for rimming a glass. This will be used in the infused rimming salt recipes in the Garnishes chapter. We buy Maldon sea salt flakes in bulk. We're also partial to local purveyors San Juan Island Sea Salt.

Vinegars: Five percent distilled white vinegar and apple cider vinegar will do to start; you may also want to pick up Champagne vinegar and red wine vinegar. We use Bragg Organic Apple Cider Vinegar, which is raw and unfiltered, so the enzymes and healthy bacteria that promote digestive health are retained.

Spices: Buy fresh—don't rely on what's been in your pantry for unknown lengths of time. Most recipes call for whole spices, which are most affordably purchased by weight at food co-ops or online specialty stores. Burlap & Barrel is a great option for fair trade spices. We recommend you always have these spices on hand: cinnamon sticks, vanilla beans, allspice berries, peppercorns, whole cloves, whole nutmeg, and cardamom seeds.

Dried herbs, flowers, and teas: If you are not growing herbs and drying your own, you will need to purchase dried rose petals, echinacea, and chamomile flowers. You will also want to purchase the dried herbs specified in the Compound Gin recipe (page 90), if you will not be drying your own herbs. Loose dried flowers, herbs, and spices are affordably purchased from online specialty stores. Mountain Rose Herbs is a good choice. Oshala Farm in Oregon also has a nice online selection from their farm.

Eggs: Egg white adds the most beautiful, silky texture to cocktails, smoothing out the rough edges for the most elegant cocktails. Bakers may recognize this texture as similar to the beginnings of a meringue—decadent, pillowy foam formed by breaking up the proteins in egg whites through shaking. It doesn't add any "eggy" flavor, but we know that raw egg white is unappealing to some. As in a Caesar salad dressing or royal icing recipes, it is perfectly safe to consume in cocktails—perhaps even more so due to the alcohol and acidic lemon added to egg white cocktails. Poultry regulations are such that risk of harmful bacteria from egg white in cocktails is very low. If you keep backyard chickens, you have even more control and oversight on the safety of your eggs.

Aquafaba: Perfect if you prefer a substitute for egg white in cocktails. Aquafaba is the liquid from a can of chickpeas, which can mimic a frothy texture of egg whites, with minimal flavor added. It does have a faint scent, so we recommend shaking drinks that contain aquafaba in a wide-mouth glass to distribute the scent, and then serving with a pleasantly fragrant garnish, such as a fresh herb.

Heavy cream or coconut cream: Add creamy texture to drinks with heavy whipping cream or coconut cream. Full-fat dairy is important when mixing drinks with other ingredients that are acidic, such as syrups, juices, and teas. The acid can cause the proteins in milk to coagulate and curdle. While unsightly, it is perfectly safe to drink. To avoid clumping, use full-fat dairy and stir in the cream slowly.

Fresh edible flowers: Buy online or at specialty grocers, grow your own, or forage blooms to adorn your cocktails and use in recipes. Make sure to use only organically grown edible flowers in drinks. Many flowers and some herbs are grown to be ornamental and are sprayed with chemicals that are not approved for human consumption. Also, if you forage for your own flowers, be sure that before you go you know which flowers are edible and what they look like. The edible flowers chart on page 36 is a great place to start. Substituting dried flowers will not have the same results as fresh, especially for very delicate flowers like elderflower and lilac.

25

Stocking Your Liquor Cabinet

We are all about encouraging you to make your own liqueurs and infused spirits, so you need not stock a huge number of liquors. Doing so is expensive and we recognize that most homes do not feature a well-stocked bar, just a bottle or two in the freezer. We also would encourage you to collect bottles one at a time, based on the drinks you like to make or new spirits you want to try, instead of going out and buying one of each of these right away. When selecting liquor, we always recommend a bottle shop or visiting distilleries to do tastings. We've spent many fun days learning about the ingredients and production behind the spirits and discovered some of our favorite products, while supporting a local business along the way. The cocktail recipes in this book use a selection of the following base spirits. Some recipes offer more than one suggestion for the spirit, so that you are more likely to be able to use what you have and what you know you enjoy drinking. These suggestions are to make shopping national stores easier, but we also encourage supporting a brand local to you.

Vodka: Vodkas are designed to be neutral and nearly flavorless, so quality over taste is what matters in cocktails. Get a bottle over $25. Stoli is a good choice.

Gin: There are two popular styles of gin: London Dry and contemporary, or "New American." London Dry gins are more traditional and juniper-forward; we recommend a bottle of Plymouth. New American gins feature a wider range of botanical aromatics beyond juniper and may lean heavier on one note, such as "floral" or "cucumber." It's worth having a bottle of both styles. For the cocktails in this book, we like The Botanist or, locally, Astraea gins, which feature aromatics inspired by the landscapes of the Pacific Northwest. Big Gin is another good local option.

Bourbon/whiskey: Maker's Mark (try the 101), Buffalo Trace, and Four Roses are good brands for mixing cocktails at a reasonable price. Belinda loves rye whiskeys to add a punchier note to a cocktail, such as Rittenhouse Rye or Old Grand-Dad Kentucky Straight Bourbon, which has a high percentage of rye for a bourbon.

Rums: Pick up one light rum and one aged rum. We like Havana Club 3 Year (a light rum) and Añejo Clasico (an aged rum) for a good value for drink making. We also like Flor de Caña 4 Year Extra Seco and Añejo Oro.

Overproof rum: The brand Wray & Nephew works great for the bitters and tinctures recipes. The higher proof is useful to speed the infusion process and pull out a deeper flavor. Substitution options are noted in the recipes.

Orange liqueur: We recommend Cointreau. Don't get the cheapest triple sec (sometimes dyed orange), if you can help it.

Nonalcoholic spirits: The expanding interest in nonalcoholic drinking has brought many new options to the market. We recommend buying these zero-proof spirits in small sizes of 375 ml or less, in order to try and find varieties you like before the shelf life of the spirit expires. Dry liquor stores that sample products are a great place to start looking. Check best-by dates and consider that their shelf lives are significantly shorter than alcohol.

Drink Crafting Techniques

Measuring: You have to measure, using a jigger for accuracy. This is not a measure-from-your-heart scenario. Bartending is like baking: precise

measurements matter a lot for the end result to be right. A finished drink may only be 4 ounces, so every bit counts to achieve a balanced taste, and just ½ ounce will alter a drink significantly. Pour right up to the rim or the measurement line of the jigger for best accuracy.

Mixing: Always follow written instructions in the recipes for shaking or stirring, and follow the timing noted for the shaking time. In general, drinks are stirred when no fresh juice or fruit is involved. The method matters for both texture and dilution. Shaken cocktails get a more aerated and light texture, whereas stirred drinks are silkier. The length of time spent shaking or stirring will also dictate how much water leaves the ice and dilutes the cocktail, which is necessary to keep your cocktails from tasting harsh or overly diluted.

Dry shake: When a very aerated texture and a lot of silky foam are desired for your drink, use a dry shake technique. Combine all the ingredients in the cocktail shaker without ice, cap firmly (shaking with ice creates a cold vacuum and helps seal the shaker, so shaking without it may cause your shaker to leak at this stage), and shake for the recipe's dictated length of time. The first shake is like a head start and builds the texture before extra water from ice is added. Next, for a second shake, add ice to the shaker, cap it, then shake again. The second shake dilutes and chills the cocktail and continues to build on the texture.

Straining: Most recipes in this book call for a simple strain to remove citrus pulp, fruit seeds, or small pieces of herbs. You can use either a Hawthorne strainer (preferred), or the built-in strainer on your cocktail shaker (these can leak or be difficult to separate; see Equipment and Pantry List, page 22). Sometimes, a fine strain is called for. A fine strain is when you use the built-in strainer on your cocktail

shaker or a cobbler strainer, and then with your other hand, hold a fine-mesh strainer above the cocktail glass. The cocktail will pass through both strainers before hitting the glass, reducing pulp and removing ice shards.

Fat washing: A way of adding richness and flavor, and smoothing out the texture of a spirit. Fat washing is combining a fat, such as olive oil or coconut oil, and a spirit, shaking the container, and then chilling the mixture. The cold fat will separate from the spirit, and then can be strained off, leaving behind a silkiness and light flavor. We only get into this a couple of times in these recipes, but it's a fun technique to learn.

Juicing citrus: To get more juice from your citrus, warm it up! Let the fruit come to room temperature or microwave the citrus for 15 seconds to soften it, then rub it along a counter, pressing into the peel as you turn the fruit. Always wash fruit before slicing and juicing it. We like a simple, inexpensive handheld juicer with a built-in strainer for easy juicing and cleanup. The amount of juice released from fruit is inconsistent, so for consistency, this book will always use measurements in ounces for drink recipes rather than "juice of one lime." For example, the juiciest fruit is fresh picked in season, whereas a green fruit picked and stored in a warehouse for later ripening and shipping will yield far less juice. Citrus for the mixer recipes (such as syrups or shrubs) have a larger finished volume that will be more forgiving, so for the sake of practicality, these recipes will use the measurement of the fruit instead of the volume in ounces.

Muddling: You can muddle herbs, fruits, vegetables, and edible flowers to add a pure flavor to a drink with minimal effort. Want to add an herbal note to a drink but have only basic spirits and a plain syrup? Muddling in a fresh thyme sprig will do the trick! Cocktail muddling tools come in handy, but a wooden spoon also works. Before muddling, always clap delicate herbs (such as mint) to release the oils from the veins of the leaves into the drink, and then stir them gently or shake them in a cocktail shaker with ice, rather than muddling them harshly with a tool. If the leaves are broken down too far, the taste can go bitter. Sturdier-stemmed herbs, such as rosemary, can withstand a strong muddle. When muddling ingredients, you may want to strain the drink so large pieces, fruit skins, and stems do not remain. Or serve the drink with a straw so that the texture of the muddled pieces is still visually interesting, but remains easy to drink around.

Canning

We often water bath can ingredients for longer storage. Water bath canning is a method of food preservation for acidic foods that uses pressure, created by boiling water and sealing lids, to create an environment within glass jars that prevents harmful bacteria from growing on the food. Only some of the drinks whose recipes we provide in this book have high enough acidity to be appropriate for preserving with a water bath canning method. The recipes for these drinks will include canning notes, such as the recipes for Fresh-Pressed Apple Cider (page 114), Fresh Tomato Juice (page 117), Citrus Cordial (page 59), and Cranberry Rosemary Syrup (page 65). However, these drinks should be water bath canned only if they have been tested with a pH meter (affordably bought online) and adjusted as necessary by adding acid, such as lemon juice, to have a pH below 4.6. Less acidic foods, such as the low-acid syrup recipes, can be safely preserved through pressure canning. Please always follow canning and preserving instructions from a reputable source, such as the National Center for Food

Preservation (nchfp.uga.edu) or your own local university's agricultural extension (we work with the agricultural extension of Washington State University, anr.cw.wsu.edu).

Infusing

Infusing is done by steeping an ingredient into a solvent, such as sugar water, vinegar, or liquor, until the solvent absorbs the flavor. Infusing is an art, not a science. The nuance of flavors can turn a very simple recipe into something very special. I aim for a flavor that is right on the edge of too much. I find that assertive infusions help each component shine and come through once they are mixed within a cocktail. Combining more than three flavors is not recommended for beginners, as the flavors easily become "muddy," or unidentifiable.

Hot infusions: Hot infusions should be done gently, with lots of tasting as you go, to get the best flavor. Use low to medium heat on a stovetop, not a microwave, to better control the process and prevent scorching. The timing of the infusion for each ingredient will vary, so taste until you reach a flavor you're happy with. Don't walk away when you're infusing something for the first time, as it can change quickly. Remember as you taste that flavors are more pronounced when hot and will be more subtle when they are chilled, so take it a little further than you maybe think you should.

Cold infusions: Cold infusions are helpful when a very delicate flavor is being extracted, such as florals. Gently coaxing the flavor out at room temperature or cold can allow for a "cleaner" flavor result. Some recipes, such as a sugar and vinegar shrub, will infuse over a series of weeks. Others, such as a hot pepper in vodka, can reach full strength in 24 hours.

29

INFUSION GUIDE

Final timing will depend on flavor preference, heat levels, freshness, and the produce and spices used. Keep notes of each infusion's measurements and infusion time.

Ingredient	Infusion Time for Syrups, Cordials, and Teas	Infusion Time for Spirits, Tinctures, and Bitters	Tips
Vanilla bean	5 to 10 minutes	1 to 2 hours	Save money by scraping the beans and using them in a recipe, then using the pod itself for infusions. Vanilla is strong, and there will be enough beans that are still clinging to the pod to give strong vanilla flavor.
Lavender	3 to 5 minutes	1 to 2 hours	Wash or shake, but don't bother removing the stems; you can dip the whole plant in upside down, buds first. This saves you time and cleanup, and the stems won't add off flavors. Taste lavender frequently to prevent a soapy, overbearing flavor.
Delicate fresh florals, such as roses, elderflower, lilac, violets	At room temperature, 24 to 48 hours	At room temperature, 48 hours or more	Infuse low and slow— delicate florals do not love high heat. Gently wash or shake, but don't bruise or rinse delicate flowers, at risk of removing the scent and flavor. Remove petals from sepals and stems to prevent bitter flavors.
Hot peppers	5 to 10 minutes	1 to 2 hours	Rough chop peppers and include the entire pepper, veins and seeds included, for the most heat. Taste frequently to avoid over-bearing heat. Pay attention to Scoville units of peppers to choose an appropriate heat for the recipe you use.
Star anise	3 to 5 minutes	up to 24 hours	Toast the spice over heat to bloom it before infusing. Taste frequently to avoid an overbearing flavor.
Fresh delicate herbs, such as cilantro, mint, lemon balm	5 to 10 minutes	1 to 3 days	Wash or shake, but don't bother removing the stems, as these also hold mild flavor. Clap herbs between your hands before dropping in to release the oils in the leaf veins. Infusions will have a purer flavor at low to no heat.
Sturdy fresh herbs, such as rosemary, thyme, sage	5 to 10 minutes	2 to 5 days	Wash well as the stems hold dirt, but don't bother removing the stems. They won't enhance the infusion but won't hurt it, either.
Citrus peels	10 to 15 minutes	1 to 3 days	Try to remove the bitter white pith if possible. Grating citrus zest or finely cutting it into julienne strips will increase infusion speed.
Fresh berries	10 to 15 minutes	3 to 5 days	Cut off green parts and remove berry stems before infusing so you can eat the soaked berries later, and gently muddle fruit for a faster infusion. Soaked fruit can be eaten as a snack or dessert if prepared this way.
Melons	Instead of infusing, juice and add the juice directly to the base recipe.	3 to 5 days	Cut off skins before infusing so you can eat the soaked melon later; watermelon soaked in tequila makes a great snack or dessert! Gently muddle fruit for a faster infusion. Alternatively, manually extract the juice or blend the melon with a small amount of water to puree them. Then fine strain the juice to remove the pulp and seeds before adding it to your recipe.
Fresh ginger	10 to 15 minutes	1 week	Grate, peel, or roughly chop ginger to expose more surface area and speed infusions.

Ingredient	Infusion Time for Syrups, Cordials, and Teas	Infusion Time for Spirits, Tinctures, and Bitters	Tips
Spruce and pine needles	10 to 15 minutes	1 to 3 days	Strip needles from branches and wash before infusing. The younger the needles, the fresher and more citrusy they will taste; as the needles harden on the tree, they begin to taste more of resin.
Stone fruits, such as peaches and plums	10 to 15 minutes	3 to 5 days	Always remove pits from stone fruits before infusing, as they contain trace amounts of cyanide and can make you sick. Gently macerate fruit to speed the infusion process. Then peel the fruit and dice it before infusing. Soaked fruit can be eaten as a snack or dessert if prepared this way.
Cinnamon	5 to 10 minutes	1 to 2 weeks	Break up whole cinnamon sticks, using a mallet or hammer, to expose more surface area and speed infusions. Toast the spice over heat to bloom it before infusing. Taste frequently to prevent an acrid or bitter flavor that can develop over time.
Allspice berries	5 to 7 minutes	7 to 10 days	Toast the spice over heat to bloom it before infusing. Crack whole berries, using a mallet or hammer, to expose more surface area and speed infusions.
Nuts	10 to 15 minutes	7 to 14 days	Toast nuts over heat to enhance nutty flavors. Shell and crack whole nuts to expose more surface area and speed infusions.
Dried herbs	5 to 10 minutes	7 to 14 days	Note that dried herbs take longer to infuse than fresh, and will have a different flavor. Use an infusion bag to make straining the final recipe easier.
Dried berries	10 to 15 minutes	7 to 14 days	Use an infusion bag to make straining the final recipe easier. Always cook dried elderberries to remove toxicity before infusing.
Cucumbers	Instead of infusing, juice and add the juice directly to the base recipe.	3 to 5 days	Peel and rough chop or slice cucumbers to expose surface area before infusing. Or, instead of infusing whole pieces, manually extract the juice or blend the cucumbers with a small amount of water to puree them. Then fine strain the juice to remove the pulp and seeds before adding it to your recipe.
Beets, carrots, mild peppers, and other vegetables	Instead of infusing, juice and add the juice directly to the base recipe.	5 to 7 days	Peel and roughly chop or slice vegetables to expose surface area before infusing. Or, instead of infusing whole pieces, manually extract the juice or blend the vegetables with a small amount of water to puree them. Then fine strain the juice to remove the pulp and seeds before adding it to your recipe.
Apples, pears	Instead of infusing, juice and add the juice directly to the base recipe.	5 to 7 days	Peel, core, and chop or slice to expose surface area before infusing. Soaked fruit can be eaten after as a snack or dessert if prepared this way.
Leafy greens, such as kale, chard, arugula	Instead of infusing, juice and add the juice directly to the base recipe.	1 to 3 days	Strip kale and chard leaves from the stems and gently tear. Roll in a ball in your hands to break up the leaves a little before adding them. Salad greens will dye infusions a range of yellow and green colors.
Peppercorns and other dried spices	5 to 7 minutes	3 to 7 days	Use an infusion bag to make straining the final recipe easier. Toast spices over heat to bloom them before infusing. Crack whole spices, using a mallet or hammer, to expose more surface area and speed infusions. Black pepper prepared this way will infuse faster.

THE

COCKTAIL
GARDEN

We give you permission to skip this chapter and get right to the crafting and drinking part. Gardening has snuck up and surprised us by how much we love it, but it's not for everyone or maybe it's not the right time for you, and your big brim hat wearing, delighting over the carrot you just pulled from the ground, digging in the dirt days are still a ways out in your future. That's okay—you can still reap the rewards of garden-to-glass drinking if you outsource the growing part.

If you do want to jump in and grow your own ingredients, here is where we'd start.

Edible Flowers for the Cocktail Garden

The list of edible flowers that exist is much longer than what we've included here, but after seven years of growing every edible floral variety we could get our hands on, we've learned that, while technically edible, some flowers don't earn their real estate in your cocktail garden (safflower, a brilliant yellow flower that is great for natural dying, comes to mind, with its harsh prickles that no one would want near their mouth). Other plants will give you a freebie edible flower you may never have expected, such as, if you let arugula go to seed, it will produce small, delicate yellow flowers.

This list contains varieties that we have found to be most useful in the cocktail garden, for some combination of their pleasant flavor, scent, color, and/or because their shape and size complements drinks well.

COLORFAST EDIBLE FLOWERS

These flowers not only look great fresh, but when dried, heated in a recipe, or frozen, they will not lose their color. They are beautiful year-round if you preserve them correctly and are great to use frozen in ice, dried and ground for floral sugars and salts, and pressed for garnishes. We are sure you can come up with even more fun uses!

EASY-GROWING EDIBLE FLOWERS

Any annuals that are easy to start, prolific, and self-seeding for blooms year after year with only one planting make this list. Similarly, perennials that require little feeding, pruning maintenance, and watering are considered easy growing. Beware that some varieties can become too easy to grow, depending on your climate. If they are prolific self-seeders, even desirable plants can become weeds, popping up where you don't want them. We have made notes about these fast spreaders.

Growing Essential Cocktail Garden Plants

Mint/lemon balm: Mint and lemon balm (a citrusy flavored leaf in the mint family) grow best via creeping roots (rhizomes). Because plants in the mint family love to spread, both can easily take over a large area quickly, which is why most gardeners suggest growing mint in containers. However, if you do grow these plants in containers, you should divide them every year by digging up and pulling out some of the roots and throwing them away, potting and giving them away to friends, or replanting in a new space. Mint can become root bound if grown in a container that is too small or if not divided frequently. To keep mint and lemon balm growing throughout the season, harvest regularly by trimming back the stem to just above a leaf node, and don't allow the plants to flower. Cutting the leaves back to an inch or two above the dirt encourages the plant to replenish itself instead of flowering, which would be the end of its growth cycle. This helps ensure multiple harvests over the season and an extended growing season well into fall. Mint and lemon balm also need plenty of water to stay productive through the hot summer months.

Chamomile: Chamomile is a dainty perennial plant that easily self-seeds. If you do not want chamomile to take over and spread, plant it in a pot. Chamomile can be seeded early in the spring and is always one of the first flowers to bloom in the cocktail garden. Blooms are best harvested early in the season before the flower has started to dry out. The seeds are very small and difficult to sow with precision, so the first year, start twice as many seeds than you think you'll need, then pull out, or "thin," half of the plants that emerge just as you might with carrots. Harvest and deadhead (remove dead blooms) frequently to encourage more blooms over the season.

35

EDIBLE FLOWER GUIDE

Edible Flower Common Name	Why We Love Them	Colorfast?	Easy Growing?	Use as a Fresh Garnish?	Flavor Notes
Calendula	Brightly colored orange, yellow, and red flowers for strong medicinal and culinary value. Annual that will self-seed in mild climates if left undisturbed and give you many seasons of blooms.	Yes	Yes	Look for small varieties.	Mildly flavored. Large-petaled varieties are a great choice for drying for teas (see page 122).
Lavender	Purple colored, highly fragrant perennial. See growing notes on page 40.	Yes	Yes, use cuttings or buy starts, as seeds can be difficult to start	Yes, trim stems to fit glass size	Strong flavor, only look for culinary varieties such as true English lavender, aka *Lavandula angustifolia*
Bachelor's button, aka cornflower	Prolific, bright blooms can be sourced in a variety of colors from pink, purple, blue, and even black.	Yes	Yes	Yes	No flavor, but makes a beautifully colored sprinkle in rimming sugars/salts, or fancy ice (see page 135).
Viola	Annual with a very long growing season in mild climates. Available in a wide range of rainbow colors. Harvest often to increase blooms.	Yes	They can be tricky to start from seed, but once growing are hardy and prolific.	Yes	Subtly sweet, mild lettucelike flavor, can be minty.
Roses	Highly fragrant and available in a wide range of colors. Treat petals delicately; they bruise easily.	Yes—when dried slowly in shade at room temperature.	No—roses are perennials that require pruning and are susceptible to disease, but once well established, will give years of blooms.	Use dried petals or choose smaller cottage-style roses	Damask roses and heirloom roses that are highly fragrant are best for culinary use. Petals should be removed from sepals and styles; the petals hold the most flavor.
Gomphrena, aka globe amaranth	Small, buttonlike buds in the prettiest range of pinks and purple jewel tones. Hardy, easy to harvest and freeze or dry beautifully whole.	Yes	Yes	Yes	No flavor but the flower is as beautiful dried as it is fresh.
Nasturtium	Prolific and helpful plant produces a bright bell-shaped flower now available in a big range of warm colors. Nasturtium will attract insects away from other plants, protecting them, so we plant these all over our garden.	No	Yes—a very high germination rate after sowing seeds directly in the garden.	Yes—keep stems in water until just before use or they will wilt. Shake and rinse flowers carefully, as insects love to hide in the bells.	Great taste when consumed fresh; can be difficult to capture in recipes. Adds a spicy bite.

Edible Flower Common Name	Why We Love Them	Colorfast?	Easy Growing?	Use as a Fresh Garnish?	Flavor Notes
Marigold	Brilliant color, easy to grow, and a good companion plant in the garden, particularly for tomatoes.	Yes	Yes—annual that can self-seed like a perennial if left undisturbed in mild climates.	Yes—look for dwarf varieties to use as garnishes; flower size of different species can range from 1 to 4 inches across.	Mild flavor isn't exciting in recipes but, when made into tea, marigold is said to have many medicinal uses, including aiding digestion and soothing headaches.
Borage	Bright blue flowers that grow easily. Borage is great for infused waters and as a garnish.	Yes; good for freezing but not for drying.	Yes—sow seeds directly. Annually self-seeds like a perennial, will spread all over the garden in mild climates.	Yes—1-inch or smaller buds are a perfect garnish.	Mild cucumber taste when consumed fresh; flavor does not translate well in recipes.
Chamomile	Delicious and medicinal, we like the Roman variety. See growing notes on page 35.	No	Yes—grows easily from seed. Start seeds indoors and transplant. Self-seeding in mild growing zones 4–7.	No—delicate petals will be waterlogged and wilt	Distinctive flavor with calming properties works well in a variety of recipes.
Toothache plant, aka Szechuan buzz button	A fun annual plant with a trick, for Buzz Button Gin (page 92). See growing tips on page 41.	No	No—grows directly from seed, but needs warm temperatures to germinate and will not tolerate even mild frosts. Do not attempt to plant until late spring/ early summer.	Yes—tell people to eat it as well!	Tastes mildly like spinach. The taste is not the most desirable attribute, but the buzzing effect of the plant is.
Lilac	"Nice-to-have" perennial ornamental (and tasty!) tree, if you have the space.	No	Yes, once established. Buy large, 5-gallon potted plants for an easy start. See growing tips on page 40.	Yes—pull single blossoms off the clustered branches; float 1 to 3 in the glass.	Deliciously, delicate florals.
Elderflower/ elderberry	Another "nice-to have" ornamental tree if you have the space. Find yours at a fruit nursery to avoid toxic species. Provides both berries and flowers, which are useful in drink making.	No	Yes, once established. See growing tips on page 40.	Yes, flowers only. Pull single blossoms off umbel clusters and float 1 to 3 in the drink	Flowers and berries each have a unique and delicious flavor. Follow cooking instructions for elderberries in the oxymel recipe (see page 78), as raw berries are toxic to consume.

Basil: Many varieties are available, and we suggest growing at least two: Genovese and Thai basil. The keys to growing productive basil are heat and careful harvesting. Try as we might to get an early crop of basil in the Pacific Northwest, we have learned that basil is one of those plants that's hard to rush without space to grow it in a greenhouse or hoop house. When we are patient and wait to plant until the days are long and warm, we're always rewarded with big, lush plants. The secret to keeping basil going through the summer is to prune the plant by cutting the stems above the leaf nodes, which encourages new side branches to grow. Then, harvest and use the leaves from the cuttings. Continuously cutting the top third of the plant helps produce a bushy, rather than leggy plant and keeps the plant from producing flowers. Pinch off growth just above a leaf node to force the plant to grow twice as many new ones, for fuller plants. Once the flowers go to seed, the leaves start to taste bitter. However, these flowers make a beautiful cocktail garnish!

Lavender: In our opinion, a garden is not a garden without some lavender. Choose culinary varieties, such as Munstead, for best results in recipes. A Mediterranean plant, lavender likes to be dry, which can be problematic in wetter climates. The key to growing lavender successfully in a wet climate is to keep its roots from getting too wet. On our farm, we plant lavender in raised rows and place a handful of gravel under each plant to help the water drain away from the roots. Although it takes a little bit of work to get new plants established, once they are, lavender is very easy to keep alive, and will bless you with its fragrant blooms year after year! Trimming lavender back to the old wood after the first bloom and every subsequent bloom will allow for many harvests in a season.

Fir or spruce tips: Each spring, evergreen trees sprout new growth at the end of their branches. In early spring, the growth is protected from freezing temperatures in a brown paper–like casing. As spring progresses and the temperatures warm, the bud grows and eventually sheds the casing, revealing a bright, tender, citrus-tasting bud. If left on the tree, the tip will harden, extending the branch, and will develop a traditional evergreen tree taste and smell. The key to harvesting the tips is timing. The earlier you pick them after they have shed their casing, the more delicate and citrusy they will taste. To ensure the tree continues to grow and stays healthy, it is recommended you never harvest more than one-third of the tips each year.

Elderflower: Cultivated or wild foraged, elderflower has a delicate flavor and is so complementary in cocktails that St-Germaine, the liqueur most often made with it, is referred to as "bartender's ketchup." Pick black or blue elder, not red. The flowers should be umbel shaped (flat, wide blossoms instead of conical). Pick in the morning for the strongest flavors. Harvest flowers early after blossoming for the best flavor—for us, this is late May or June, depending on the year and the climate. Pick only fresh blooms—there should be no browning, and they should be fully blossomed. Don't pick more than one-third of the flowers on a bush, because the remaining blossoms will become elderberries in fall.

Lilac: Lilacs are one of the most fragrant flowers in our cocktail garden. While most lilac plants are technically shrubs, it is not uncommon for older plants, unpruned, to grow tall like a tree. In fact, the lilac shrub at the farm is taller than the house. So, when planting a lilac plant, make sure you plan for it to get tall, or prune it regularly using the one-third rule (do not prune more than one-third of growth at a time, and the plant will be able to rebound well). Prune just after blooming to avoid reducing the following year's blooms. Most lilacs bloom in early spring. When cooking with lilac, you want to use only the petals and not the stems or green leaves, as their taste is quite bitter. The petals hold a delicate flavor that is delightful in drink syrups, floral waters, and tinctures.

40

Toothache plant: These little flowers are one of our favorite party tricks. We promise, if you grow these and bring them with you to a party, you will instantly become the most interesting person in the room. They go by many names, including buzz buttons, electric daisy, and Szechuan buzz buttons. The scientific name is *Acmella oleracea*. When eaten, the plant has a tantalizing effect on your mouth. While everyone describes the sensations differently, most people experience a combination of tingling, numbing, and salivating. Toothache plants are a perennial in climates where the average temperature is 80°F, which means they prefer nice, warm weather. Don't bother starting them before the weather is hot, or they won't germinate or grow well. Once they're growing well, harvest and deadhead (remove old blooms) frequently to encourage new growth.

Rosemary: Rosemary is one of the most easily recognized herbs in our cocktail garden and in our recipes. In recipes, the distinctive flavor instantly makes itself known, and in the garden, rosemary is the most fragrant herb we grow. There is nothing like the smell of walking through a freshly pruned row of rosemary. Like lavender, rosemary is a Mediterranean herb that likes to be hot and dry. However, there are varieties that are well adapted to colder climates. On the farm, we have planted both Madeline Hill and Arp varieties, and have found Madeline Hill to be the best at withstanding cold temperatures. To keep the size of a rosemary bush controlled, trim it back to just above the old wood a couple of times per season.

Fennel: Fennel is a plant that is usually sold as a bulb in grocery stores and at farmers' markets, so if you haven't grown it yourself, you might not know it can get up to 6 feet tall and has the most prolific canopy of umbel flowers. All parts of the plant are edible. The flowers attract a wide variety of pollinators, including bees, wasps, and lacewings. The seeds have a strong anise or licorice taste and are often used to flavor Italian sausage, but they also make delicious cocktail infusions. If you decide to grow fennel in your cocktail garden, take note, it very easily self-seeds in moderate growing zones, and at 6 feet tall, it is very hard to control where the seeds will land. It can take over, so take care to trim back your fennel regularly, and consider planting it in containers. Don't plant fennel near tomatoes, bush beans, peas, or eggplant. We isolate it in a pot in a corner of the garden.

Pruning and Harvesting

Keeping annuals healthy: Most true annuals and self-seeding annuals benefit from frequent harvesting and deadheading. Harvest flowers by gently plucking them from the stems. Deadhead (remove dead blooms) frequently to encourage new growth.

Keeping perennials healthy: Perennial flowers, such as lilacs and elderflowers, form buds the year before and will bloom only once over the season. Cutting off dead blooms will keep the plant happy, but will not encourage new growth in the same season. Only prune these shrubs immediately after flowering, before the new buds form, or you will be reducing the blooms for the following season. If you want to reshape your edible shrubs, remove dead wood, or reduce height; cut no more than one-third of foliage each year.

Harvesting flowers for use in recipes: Florals work best in recipes when the flowers are freshly bloomed and strongly scented. Pick flowers on a dry morning when their scent is strongest and let them sit on a counter or in a tray so that garden friends can escape before you start removing the stems from the flowers. Do not rinse the flowers and make the recipe as soon as possible for best results. The organic compounds that are responsible for a flower's scent are volatile and begin to lose their potency as soon as the flower is clipped and brought inside, so timing matters in order to best capture the delicate floral flavors. Most floral flavors are concentrated on the petals, so you will remove the stamen, styles, and stems (all the green parts) before cooking with them.

Harvesting woody herbs: Trimming these plants is essential to keep them happy year after year, and will encourage new growth within the same year. In the case of lavender, it will encourage several blooms over a season. Trim back sage, lavender, thyme, and rosemary plants by no more than one-third at a time, and never cut into the old stem wood or else the plant will be susceptible to illness and will not grow back. If flowers are left to die on the stem, the plant will stop producing for the season and the base will become scraggly and woody.

Harvesting delicate herbs: Basil, calendula, carnation, gomphrena, celosia, oregano, tarragon, sage, and marigold all do better if you give the plants a regular pinch. These plants start by growing on one central stem, but by cutting back the stem to half after it reaches at least 6 inches of growth, you can promote the growth of more side arms. When you pinch off leaves, new leaves will grow doubly. Then, as the plant grows, continue to pinch off the top sets of leaves to encourage more blooms. This will create a bushier, fuller plant with more leaves to harvest. Whatever you pinch off can be used in a recipe!

Planning Your Garden

Venise grows in tilled rows on an acre on the farm as well as in a raised bed garden where new plants and varieties are tested. She plants a wide range of flowers and herbs in addition to tomatoes, peppers, tomatillos, garlic, onions, beets, potatoes, pickling and salad cucumbers, peas, bush beans, rhubarb, and blueberries, and the farm has a few pie cherry, heirloom apple, and pear trees, as well as lilac, fir, and spruce trees to forage from.

Belinda grows her garden in four raised beds and randomly in spaces around her yard in ornamental beds. Edible plants are often ornamental and many herbs spread, so they're a great way to reduce weeding and bring in that loosely romantic, English cottage garden look.

If you have no other space, plant a small collection of your favorite herbs on a windowsill or in a small container garden on a patio. Having fresh herbs at your fingertips will be hugely impactful to your recipes.

Every year, we change up what we grow slightly to fit our drink interest and moods (seed catalogs are a new kind of shopping addiction), and based on what we learned the season before. Take notes throughout the season on what you enjoyed growing, used the most, and the plants that grew the best for you each year. Gardeners don't have to constantly pivot or iterate to improve—we get a growing season stretch of time to learn from our successes and failures and then we try again next year. Every year our gardens teach us something new.

You don't need a ton of space to start a small cocktail garden. If you show restraint and plant only one or two starts of each and ignore spacing rules (totally fine to do as long as your soil has enough water and nutrients; you keep on top of pruning to ensure the plants all have enough sunlight and airflow; and you don't plant them on top of one another), you can fit most of the essential plants listed on pages 35 to 41 in pots on a typical home patio or in a raised bed garden.

For example, here we have a 4 × 4–foot garden bed plus a couple of pots for plants that spread the easiest and will overtake your garden space.

Then, plant the rest in a single raised bed, densely planted, using vertical supports as needed to allow vining plants to grow up instead of spread out.

The example garden bed layout opposite does not contain every plant we recommend, but it does have the majority of our favorite plants for drink making. The layout considers companion-planting needs and benefits, height, and color for

PLANTING A 4' X 4' COCKTAIL GARDEN

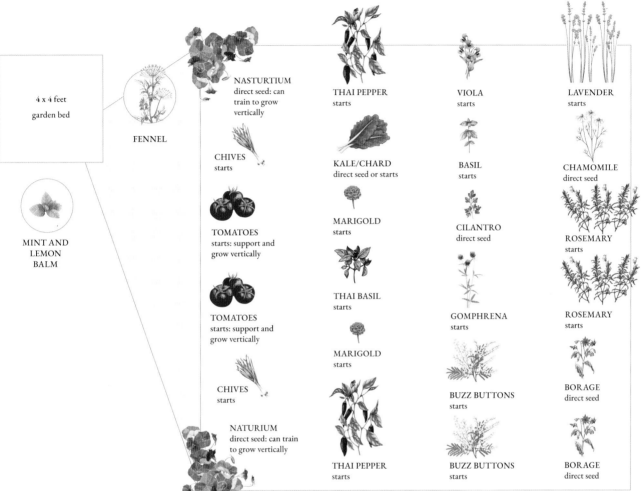

4 x 4 feet
garden bed

FENNEL

MINT AND
LEMON
BALM

NASTURTIUM
direct seed: can
train to grow
vertically

CHIVES
starts

TOMATOES
starts: support and
grow vertically

TOMATOES
starts: support and
grow vertically

CHIVES
starts

NATURIUM
direct seed: can train
to grow vertically

THAI PEPPER
starts

KALE/CHARD
direct seed or starts

MARIGOLD
starts

THAI BASIL
starts

MARIGOLD
starts

THAI PEPPER
starts

VIOLA
starts

BASIL
starts

CILANTRO
direct seed

GOMPHRENA
starts

BUZZ BUTTONS
starts

BUZZ BUTTONS
starts

LAVENDER
starts

CHAMOMILE
direct seed

ROSEMARY
starts

ROSEMARY
starts

BORAGE
direct seed

BORAGE
direct seed

43

a functional and beautiful layout for your cocktail garden. It places perennial and self-seeding annual herbs on the outsides so that they are easy to work around if supplementing or turning over soil, and can come back year after year.

Plant perennials and self-seeding annuals in areas where you can let them come back year after year, such as garden rows that will not be tilled or in an ornamental area of your lawn. You can also grow them potager style, in the outside edges of a raised garden bed, as we are recommending here. If you do so, label the area carefully so you remember not to turn over the soil deeply in that area and risk disturbing the seeds. Just supplement with mulch and organic fertilizer as needed.

We have noted for each plant whether we directly sow seeds in the soil or we recommend buying starts (small plants that have been started indoors or in a greenhouse to grow strong and get a head start on the season before being planted out in the garden). For the nasturtium, we recommend planting seeds directly in the ground in your garden bed's corners and letting their beautiful flowers spill over the container's edge.

SYRUPS

AND

CORDIALS

yrups and cordials are used in cocktail recipes to provide lift and depth of flavor. While many of these recipes utilize fresh juice, produce, herbs, and spices to build a drink's flavor in addition to sugar—few drinks we include would be categorized as "sweet" cocktails—most of them do include a small amount of syrup or cordial. Sugar is an important tool in cocktail making to bring balance to drinks.

There are a lot of ways to reduce sugar in your diet, but cocktail recipes are not the best place to try. The majority of sugar in a cocktail comes from the spirits themselves—approximately 100 to 150 calories per shot—whereas the calories in a cocktail from added sugar may clock in from 15 to 50 calories. The small amount of sweetness, enjoyed in moderation, is essential to bring out other flavors and help your cocktails taste better.

Made from a 50/50 ratio of sugar and water and flavored in any number of ways, a simple syrup is a common "sweet" element in a balanced cocktail. A simple syrup is a workhorse recipe to have up your sleeve. Many classic cocktails call for a sweetening component in the form of sugar syrups, and almost always, anywhere a cocktail recipe calls for sugar, honey, or even grenadine, a simple syrup can be substituted.

Sometimes, a particular texture is called for in a drink recipe and you will see a call for a "rich syrup" or a specific sugar, such as brown sugar, turbinado sugar, or even maple sugar. A "rich syrup" may be a familiar term for those familiar with canning and preserving, and in those contexts is a 2:1 recipe instead of the 1:1 recipe we'll use here. The particulars of these syrups is getting into the bartending weeds, and while we gardeners know weeds are inevitable, they are not necessary, either. In most drinks, and certainly for most circumstances you'll find yourself drinking them in, a simple syrup will work just fine.

A cordial is a type of concentrated syrup that is fruit or citrus juice based, instead of water based as in a simple syrup. They are a method of preserving fresh juice that should be used to complement, not replace, fresh juices in a cocktail recipe. The term sometimes refers to liqueurs, but in the United States, cordials can also be a nonalcoholic beverage syrup. Cordials are an excellent way of preserving floral syrups, because the added acidity of citrus juice will lower the pH and allow the syrup to keep longer in the fridge.

Both simple syrups and cordials can take a classic, familiar cocktail recipe and turn it into something of Simple Goodness. Despite having made these professionally for seven years, we've only begun scraping the wooden spoon around the inside of the syrup pot—there are so many delicious combinations yet to try.

BASIC FLAVORED SIMPLE SYRUP

Makes about 12 ounces

1 cup granulated cane sugar

1 cup water

½ cup washed and roughly chopped fruit, berries, and/or vegetables

Aromatics, such as spices or herbs—begin with a couple of teaspoons for stronger flavors, such as peppercorns, and up to ¼ cup for subtle flavors, such as mint or sage

TIP
Measure syrup in 1-ounce portions (or your most used measurement) into an ice cube tray and freeze. This is a great make-ahead for warm weather parties, so you can mix drinks quickly for a group. Do not store syrups in an uncovered ice cube tray long term, or the flavor will absorb other flavors from your freezer.

STORAGE TIP
Store in the fridge for up to 2 months, depending on the flavor (syrups with acidic ingredients added such as lemon or cranberry allow for a longer refrigerated storage life, while plain sugar and water syrups tend to last a few weeks to a month) and how many solids remain in the syrup after straining—the more solid pieces there are, the greater the chance of developing mold.

This recipe can be amended for any season and any produce you've harvested. It can bring seasonality and intrigue to drinks in a single step—try making squash syrups, cucumber syrups, floral syrups, and spice syrups.

Combine the sugar and water in a saucepot over medium heat. Stir until the sugar dissolves. Do not let the mixture come to a rolling boil. When the sugar is dissolved, lower the heat to a low simmer and add your fruit, berries, and/or vegetables to infuse.

THERE ARE A COUPLE OF WAYS TO DO THIS:
1. Add these ingredients directly. As they begin to heat and soften, you may want to mash the fruit or other additions with the back of a wooden spoon to speed the breakdown process and release their juices.

2. Place them in tea bags, cheesecloth, or mesh tea balls before adding them to the pot. This requires more equipment and creates additional cleanup, but can make infusing much simpler and less messy. Use one ingredient per receptacle. This is especially important if you plan to make a syrup with more than one flavor, because ingredients will infuse at different strengths and should be removed at different times. For instance, berries or apples may remain in the pot for 20 minutes, whereas mint will need only 5 minutes or less over low heat to infuse before turning bitter.

When the desired flavor is reached, remove the pan from the heat and use a funnel and a fine-mesh strainer to strain out all solids. Then, transfer the syrup to a clean glass jar with a tight-fitting lid. Mason jars or recycled and cleaned vinegar and sauce bottles work well.

NOTE: Whenever you make a syrup with fresh herbs or flowers, you could choose to steep them first in this recipe's water, then strain them before adding your sweetener. This makes whatever you use to strain less sticky and much easier to clean up. But this is why we do not recommend it: your palate. Infusing the sweetened syrup with the flowers directly allows you to develop a sense of the strength of infusion needed. It is harder to guess at the desired flavor of individual components before you combine them, and will be more exact to taste the finished product and know you've reached your desired taste. This (and the added mess of cleaning a blender and strainer) is also why we don't include recipes for blender syrups in this book.

STRAWBERRY SYRUP

Makes about 12 ounces

1 cup granulated cane sugar

1 cup water

1 cup strawberries, washed and hulled

Use this syrup in Strawberries and Cream Soda (page 163), Fresh Lemonade by the Pitcher (page 168), Dirty Soda (page 174), Pitcher Punch (page 221), or Smash (page 215).

You've got to pick your own strawberries at least once in your life. Our kids always choose to grow strawberries in the raised bed gardens they control on the farm, because strawberries are their favorite snacks, and with gardening, you should really prioritize growing what you love to eat. U-Pick at a berry farm is another fun, and sadly dwindling, way to bring home a basket of the tastiest strawberries while having a good time. It's worth seeking out your nearest U-Pick farm online, packing up some car snacks, and heading out to the dusty fields. You'll be bending your way down the rows, breaking your back for these little red gems, and at the end, you will feel sore but satisfied. Am I selling it yet? It's a very specific brand of fun, one I highly recommend. You're going to snack on berries on the ride home as you watch the farmland pass by, so make sure you get enough for both eating and making a big batch of this syrup.

Combine the sugar and water in a saucepot over medium heat, then add the berries and mash them as they heat to release their juices. Stir often to dissolve the sugar. Once the sugar has dissolved and the berries are finely mashed and juicy, remove from the heat. Strain out the berry pulp and seeds.

Bottle in a clean container with a lid, and store in the refrigerator for up to 2 months.

NOTE: You can substitute any berry in this recipe.

BLACKBERRY
AND
MINT SYRUP

Makes about 12 ounces

1 cup marionberries or blackberries

1 cup granulated cane sugar

1 cup water

½ cup fresh mint—use young, soft mint leaves without any browning, for best flavor

Use this syrup in a cocktail: our favorite Iced Tea (page 170), Marionberry Mojito (page 210), Southside (page 213), or Smash (page 215).

Blackberries ripen beginning in August where we live, which tends to be the hottest month on the farm, when our mint begins to struggle to keep enough water under the sun's relentless shining. We always do a big trim of the mint right around Belinda's birthday (August 16), which is the same time that the berries are ripe on the drive up to the farm—so we go out with the kids in the cooler evenings and mornings to pick.

The timing of these mint cuttings—while ripe, dark berries were draining in colanders in the sink—first inspired this syrup flavor.

Combine the berries with the sugar and water in a saucepot over medium heat and mash the berries as they heat to release their juices. Stir often to dissolve the sugar. Once the sugar has dissolved and the berries are finely mashed and juicy, remove from the heat and add the mint. Infuse the mint off the heat for 5 to 10 minutes, tasting as you go until the mint flavor is round and present but not bitter.

Strain out the mint and berry seeds.

Bottle in a clean container with a lid, and store in the refrigerator for up to 2 months.

NOTE: You can use any berry in this recipe and any variety of mint, though we like spearmint. The mint can also be replaced with lemon balm, which works well.

51

SPRUCE
(OR FIR)
TIP SYRUP

Makes about 12 ounces

1 cup granulated cane sugar

1 cup water

½ cup freshly picked and budded
spruce tips (see harvesting tip,
page 40)

1 lemon, cut in half and juiced

Use this syrup in a cocktail:
Fresh Lemonade by the Pitcher
(page 168), Nonalcoholic Buck
(page 167) Sun Tea (page 126),
Spruce Drop (page 204), or
Coastal Collins (page 198).

Spruce trees grow all along the back pasture at the farm, providing tree cover for the cows in the heat of summer and a pretty snowy landscape during winter. A Pacific Northwest winter is a marathon, in which we're preparing garden beds for the following spring, planting seeds in the greenhouse, and all the while trying to keep our seasonal depression tamped down as the sky bears down on us daily: gray, heavy, full of clouds. Spruce and fir tips emerge each year in May in a period Northerners call "false summer," when the sky opens up bright and blue and the trees push out their new growth in lime green Technicolor. To forgo harvesting the tips, the offerings that say, "Don't worry, summer is coming!" would feel like an insult to the weather.

Harvested when the tips first emerge from their papery casings, the needles taste bright and citrusy. Spruce and Douglas fir are both delightful, oft-overlooked ingredients in a modern kitchen that Native Americans used medicinally. Western settlers learned to brew the vitamin C–rich tips as a tea to keep scurvy at bay after a long winter without fresh produce. The brewed tips give an energy boost referred to as Nature's Gatorade. This syrup is our nod to the trees that are an important component of the traditional diet of Coastal Salish people.

This syrup is brilliant with gin, sherry, vermouth, and vodka cocktails and pairs nicely with citrus.

Combine the sugar and water in a small saucepot over medium heat. Stir to dissolve the sugar. After the sugar has dissolved into the syrup, add the spruce tips and infuse over low to medium heat for 20 minutes, tasting as you go until a lemony flavor is developed.

Add the lemon juice to enhance the citrusy flavor and extend the life of the syrup. Strain out the tips and any lemon seeds. Bottle in a clean container with a lid, and store in the refrigerator for up to 2 months.

53

LIME BASIL SYRUP

Makes about 12 ounces

½ cup basil of choice

1 cup granulated cane sugar

1 cup water

Zest and juice of 2 limes

> A natural friend for vodka, gin, tequila, and rum cocktails, Lime Basil Syrup also brightens limeade, sodas, and iced herbal teas. Use it in Back Porch Lemonade (page 219) and Cucumber Basil Gimlet (page 216).

Born out of a bumper crop of basil one summer, this syrup can be incorporated into a wide variety of drinks, especially any drink recipe featuring fresh citrus juices and clear spirits. The lime juice brings brightness to balance out the sweet, floral basil and will help the syrup keep longer in the fridge as well. Basil lemonade, basil margaritas, basil gin and tonics, basil vodkatinis . . . you really should use this one liberally! Basil isn't a common flavor in the beverage market, but after you make this syrup, you'll wonder why you haven't been drinking more of it. The natural sweetness of the herb softens alcohol beautifully.

For the best flavor, use soft, fresh basil leaves without any browning or flowers formed. Basil has a range of flavors from lemon to chocolate, Thai to Italian. For example, Thai basil is sweeter and mintier, whereas Genovese basil is more savory. Consider which notes you want to complement in a cocktail when choosing your basil. Or use whatever you grew—we bet it will taste pretty good regardless!

Remove the basil leaves from the stems.

Combine the sugar and water in a saucepot over medium heat, stirring often to dissolve the sugar. Once the sugar has dissolved, add the lime zest. Add the lime juice to the pot and stir (it is okay if you get a seed in there; it will be strained out). Remove the pot from the heat, then add the basil leaves. Infuse the basil off the heat for 5 to 10 minutes, tasting as you go, until the basil flavor is round and present. Left too long in the syrup, basil will become bitter and vegetal in taste.

Strain the syrup through a fine-mesh strainer to remove all the basil and any lime seeds. Bottle in a clean container with a lid, and store in the refrigerator for up to 2 months.

LAVENDER HONEY SYRUP

Makes about 12 ounces

1 cup raw honey

¾ cup water

2 tablespoons fresh lavender buds

Pair Lavender Honey Syrup with gin, vodka, and whiskey cocktails, and drink it in Creamy Tea Cobbler (page 173), Fresh Lemonade by the Pitcher (page 168), Old-Fashioned (page 188), and Iced Tea (page 170).

Lavender Honey Syrup preserves the sweetness of summer for use all year long. We cut back and regrow our lavender plants throughout summer to increase our harvest yield, and if we time it just right, the last cutting falls at the end of September. We love making this honey syrup when the nights begin cooling off and we know we're savoring the last of the lavender blooms. The syrup can also be made in summer when the buds are fresh, or any time in the year using dried lavender flowers, if you follow the dehydrating instructions on page 122. In summertime, use the syrup in sweet lemonades and bright, refreshing cocktails, and keep making it in fall and winter for cozy coffee drinks and hot toddies.

Local honey has many health benefits, including boosting immunity, so this is a great fit to add to drinks as the seasons cool and germs begin to spread.

Shake the lavender stems to remove any garden friends. Remove the lavender buds from the stems by pulling down the stem, then measure.

Combine the measured honey and water in a small saucepan. Add the lavender buds, using a mesh tea ball if you have one for easier cleanup.

Heat over medium-low heat, stirring gently to prevent crystallizing the honey or having the heat zap it of some of its natural benefits (raw honey is the best for you). Once the honey has dissolved, taste often. The infusion likely only needs 3 to 4 minutes with fresh lavender; you want the lavender flavor to be present, but not too strong or "soapy." Remove the pot from the heat. Strain the syrup, if needed, through a fine-mesh strainer to remove all the lavender buds.

Bottle in a clean container with a lid, and store in the refrigerator for up to 2 months.

57

OLEO SACCHARUM WITH HERBS

Makes about 8 ounces

2 oranges

2 lemons

1 grapefruit

2 sprigs rosemary

1 sprig tarragon

3 sprigs thyme or lemon verbena

1 cup granulated cane sugar

Use to sweeten and flavor Iced Tea (page 170), Fresh Lemonade by the Pitcher (page 168), Old-Fashioned (page 188), Pitcher Punch (page 221), or Hot Toddy (page 242).

A sweet syrup made by extracting flavor from the oils of citrus rinds, an oleo saccharum holds intense sour flavor. It's an efficient way to use all the citrus peels you collect after making cocktails. Here, we're also using garden herbs and letting sugar and acid pull flavor from the herb leaves. The sour flavor of an oleo saccharum is very concentrated and, because it's preserved with sugar, it will not break down and start tasting "off" over time, as freshly squeezed citrus juices do. This stable sweet-sour combination makes oleo saccharum a great option to use in punches or other large-batch cocktails that you make ahead. The finished drink can sit out for hours during a party and still taste fresh from the garden.

It is important to thoroughly scrub the citrus peels to remove any wax before you zest them, since everything will get extracted in the recipe, including any chemicals that were sprayed on the fruit.

Wash the fruits and herbs thoroughly and then zest the fruit with a Microplane grater, making sure to stop before you hit the white pith. (In other words, zest just the top layer of the skin.) Place the citrus zest aside in a small bowl.

Alternatively, if you are practicing whole-animal bartending and using citrus peels from citrus that has already been juiced, zesting will be difficult so you can do this: cut the peels in half and then lay open the citrus peels like a fillet, nice and flat. Using a sharp paring knife, place your knife sideways and shimmy it along the peel to cut off as much of the white pith as possible (it doesn't taste very good), leaving just the colorful rind. Then, simply cut the peel into very thin julienne strips.

Strip the leaves of the herbs off the stems and add the leaves to the bowl. Add the sugar and lightly toss with a spoon, to cover the herbs and citrus with the sugar. Place a dishcloth over the top of the bowl. Let it sit for an hour before stirring just once; as the oils begin to be pulled from the rind by the sugar, the sugar will start to liquefy and form a syrup. Let it sit for 2 hours, covered, at room temperature, before straining out the fruit and herb pieces and storing the syrup. Bottle in a clean glass container with a lid, and store in the refrigerator for up to 2 months.

NOTE: You can use any combination of your preferred or available citrus and herbs here. Thyme is lovely. Tarragon sits more on the edge of popularity in the herb schema, but maybe that's your brand and you love the unexpected—go for it! Licorice-like herbs, such as hyssop, also work nicely but have a smaller fan base.

CITRUS CORDIAL

Makes about 12 ounces

8 limes, 6 lemons, 4 oranges, or 2 grapefruits, or a combination of these, to yield 8 ounces of juice

About 8 ounces sugar

This syrup is used in the nonalcoholic Cordial Spritz (page 169), pairs with every spirit, and is excellent for a Sparkling Rosé Wine Spritzer (page 182), a beer shandy, such as the Making Hay Shandy (page 187), and White Sangria (page 194).

Winter citrus is the bright light at the end of a Pacific Northwest winter. We look forward to California's citrus hitting the market at the dreary time of year here where the gray skies seem to stretch on forever, the garden is a sad tangle of last year's plants left to self-seed, and we live vicariously through the year's first seed catalogs arriving in the mail. Then comes a cascade of citrus from the south, from the usual to exotic: blood oranges, tangelos, and pomelos all bring new drink inspiration.

A cordial is another way of making a syrup. It is similar to oleo saccharum because it begins with the oil of citrus peels and sugar extracting flavor until it all melts into a thick and flavorful syrup, but for a cordial, you also add fresh citrus juice. You'll want to use equal parts sugar and juice.

Zest the fruit with a Microplane grater, taking care to turn the peels evenly all the way around, so you get the most zest from the rinds. Then, slice the fruit in half and juice them. Discard the rinds. Measure the juice and add an equal amount of sugar, then stir in the zest. Cover and let stand for 24 hours, stirring a couple of times so that the sugar doesn't settle. After 24 hours, strain the cordial into a clean glass jar. Seal and store in the refrigerator for up to 2 months.

NOTE: Lemon and lime cordials have a high enough acidity that they can be safely preserved to be shelf stable through the process of water bath canning at home. See the note on canning on page 29.

59

LILAC CORDIAL

Makes 7 ounces

10 organically grown lilac clusters

5 cups granulated cane sugar

4 cups boiling water

Handful of blueberries, for color (optional)

2 lemons

Pairs particularly well with gin and vodka, and is excellent for a Sparkling Rosé Wine Spritzer (page 182), Cordial Spritz (page 169), and makes Lilac and Lead French 75 (page 185).

Lilacs sit right outside each of our front doors and signal the start of summer with their blooms every time we step off our porches. The scent is powerful and nostalgic. It isn't enough to cut the blooms and pop them in bud vases all over the house, we want to drink them, too! For this reason, lilacs were one of the first flowers ever used in our experiments with drinks. Belinda first used this syrup in 2016 in a French 75 variation called Lilac and Lead (page 185). While lilacs may be prevalent in your neighborhood, yard care chemicals last for years in plants, so take care to follow the growing instructions on page 40 to keep your drinks healthy.

You can add a few blueberries to mimic a lilac's light purple if your blooms don't color your syrup. Lilacs have a short season and will work best in recipes when the flowers are freshly bloomed and strongly scented.

Prepare the lilacs by shaking them to remove garden friends. Do not rinse the flowers, or you will remove the flavor from the petals. Pull the lilac flowers from their stems, making sure that only the delicate flowers make it into the syrup and taking care to discard any green pieces, which will add bitterness. Set the flowers aside.

Place the sugar in a stockpot of boiling water and stir to dissolve the sugar into a syrup. Once dissolved, remove the syrup from the heat. Add the blueberries (if using), then crush the berries to release their color. Zest the lemons and add the zest to the syrup, then slice and squeeze the lemon juice into the syrup. If any seeds get in, it is okay, because you will strain the syrup later.

Add the prepared lilac buds to the syrup. Cover the pot with a lid or clean towel and let the cordial stand at room temperature for 1 to 2 days, stirring a couple of times daily. Taste, and when the floral flavor is strong but not bitter, strain the cordial through cheesecloth or a fine-mesh strainer. Pour into a clean glass bottle, label, seal, and store in the refrigerator for up to 2 months.

FORAGED ELDERFLOWER CORDIAL

Makes about 24 ounces

5 cups granulated cane sugar

4 cups boiling water

2 lemons

12 to 15 elderflower heads, stalk and all green pieces removed

Add it everywhere, as this syrup brightens drinks beautifully and pairs particularly well with citrus. Use for the Cordial Spritz (page 169), Nonalcoholic Buck (page 167), and Back Porch Lemonade (page 219).

Many a mountain roadside drive has been paused with Belinda getting out of the car to harvest elderflowers from the brilliant white bushes that grow abundantly in our area. Once you've identified wild elderflower trees, which are native to Europe and grow well in mild climates, you will see them everywhere. They're easiest to spot in early summer when in bloom with big umbel clusters of tiny white flowers, and then you can return to the same trees to forage again in fall for the berries. The berries are said to have medicinal value for boosting immunity in cold and flu season, while the flowers smell and taste like heaven itself. Belinda is more obsessed with the flowers for the purpose of making this cordial. Timing matters to get aromatics from the flowers into syrup and to capture the strong floral flavor. Harvest in the morning, do not rinse the flowers, and make the cordial the same day for best results.

Place the sugar in a stockpot of boiling water and stir to dissolve the sugar into a syrup. Once dissolved, remove the syrup from the heat. Zest the lemons and add the zest to the syrup, then slice and squeeze the lemon juice into the syrup.

Prepare the elderflowers by shaking them to remove insects. Do not rinse the flowers, or you will remove the flavor from the petals. Snip the white flower ends from the tiny green stems, using kitchen scissors. Add these white buds to the syrup, taking care to discard any green pieces.

Cover the pot with a lid or clean towel and let the cordial stand at room temperature for 1 to 2 days, stirring a couple of times daily. Taste, and when the floral flavor is strong but not bitter, strain the cordial through cheesecloth or a fine-mesh strainer. Pour into a clean glass bottle, label, seal, and store. Seal and store in the refrigerator for up to 2 months.

NOTE: This recipe has a larger yield than most of our recipes. This is because the season of opportunity to make it is short, so we make a larger batch and use a lot of it in the Elderflower Liqueur recipe (page 106).

PUMPKIN SPICE SYRUP

Makes about 12 ounces

½ small pumpkin (preferably sugar pie variety) with stem, seeds, and strings removed (or skip this step and use ½ cup canned pure pumpkin puree)

½ cinnamon stick

1 cup water

2 cups granulated sugar

½ vanilla bean

½ teaspoon grated nutmeg

Use in Iced Coffee (page 176), Hot Spiced Cider (page 175), Home for the Holidays on the Ranch (page 235), Homecoming Margarita (page 231), and Walk in the Woods (page 209) cocktails.

Our little pumpkin patch is never ready for picking in late September when the commercial pumpkin spice craze begins, but it brings us a lot of deliciousness and fun carving come late October, when the pumpkins have ripened on the vine. It's become tradition to carve the kids' names in the pumpkins early on when they are green and growing, then watch the scarred pumpkins grow and grow with their new tattoos stretching (not unlike some of ours!) as they go.

These days, pumpkin spice is in just about everything, while somehow containing only trace amounts of actual pumpkin. A true pumpkin spice syrup takes a few steps but tastes miles away from typical coffee shop syrups, which are essentially cinnamon, sugar, and water with so-called natural flavors added.

This syrup is a fantastic way to add moisture and flavor to a pumpkin sheet cake as a syrup soak between the cake and cream cheese frosting layers. We drink it in our fall drinks, such as the whiskey sour we made one year that tasted so much like a Hallmark movie scene that we had to call it Home for the Holidays on the Ranch (To Find Love), see page 235. But while there are many possible uses, if we're honest, we just make a big batch and use it in hot and iced coffees all the way through Christmas.

You can use a blend of pumpkin and squash for the syrup. If you're roasting squash for dinner and have some extra, use it to make this! Baking pumpkin pies from scratch for the holidays? It is a great saver to roast a little more than your recipe calls for, then puree and freeze the extra, and you will be ready to make this syrup for months to come!

Roast the pumpkin in the oven at 400°F for about 20 minutes, or until soft enough to scoop its flesh away from the skin. While it is roasting, prepare the cinnamon: Use a mallet, hammer, the bottom of a small cast-iron pan, or a meat tenderizer to pound the cinnamon stick into smaller pieces. Toast the cinnamon in a clean, dry pan over low heat for 30 to 60 seconds, or until fragrant.

Using a spoon, scoop out the soft flesh from the skin of the pumpkin and place the flesh in a blender or food processor along with the water, then puree until smooth. Transfer the pumpkin, cinnamon pieces, and sugar to a saucepot over medium heat and stir to dissolve the sugar.

Fillet open a vanilla bean on a cutting board, using a sharp paring knife, then scrape the vanilla out of the pod using the tip of the knife, dragging it along the pod to collect the vanilla. Add the vanilla to the pot, scraping the back of the knife on the rim of the saucepot to ensure you get as much of it as you can into the syrup. Add the nutmeg.

Continue to cook the syrup at a simmer for 5 to 10 minutes over medium-low heat, stirring to incorporate the vanilla and nutmeg, and allowing the cinnamon to infuse. Taste the syrup after 5 minutes to check whether the spices have reached their desired flavor. When you are happy with the flavor, strain the syrup through a fine-mesh strainer, pushing the pumpkin through with a rubber spatula. Discard the pulp and cinnamon pieces. Bottle the strained syrup in a clean container with a lid, and store in the refrigerator for up to 2 months.

NOTE: For less cleanup, make this a one-vessel recipe by using an immersion blender right in the saucepot, instead of a blender or food processor.

CRANBERRY ROSEMARY SYRUP

Makes about 12 ounces

2 sprigs rosemary

1 cup pure cranberry juice, no sugar added and not from concentrate

1 cup granulated cane sugar

Use in Simple Syrup Soda (page 164), Hard Seltzer or Ranch Water (page 181), Shoalwater Sea Breeze (page 244), Sparkler (page 239), and Harvest Moon Punch (page 240).

You may be wondering why we are not using the obvious shortcut here: canned cranberries. They would work for flavor, and it's always nice to have an ingredient pull double duty in the kitchen. However, whole cranberries (including those that come in cans) contain a whole lot of pectin, which is the chemical in fruits that makes them gel. This can thicken the syrup almost to the consistency of a jelly. If you use pure—not concentrated—cranberry juice (find it with natural juices or make your own by water bath canning 1½ cups of whole cranberries in a quart-size jar with water), the syrup will have a better texture for drinks.

The high acidity of cranberries make it so that this syrup pulls more than its weight in the work of balancing a cocktail—the sweet, sour, and even savory with the herbal rosemary are contained in one easy-to-use ingredient. This syrup makes a wonderful shortcut for holiday baking (do drizzle it over cheesecake!) or topping breakfast oats.

Shake the rosemary sprigs to remove any garden friends. Remove the rosemary leaves from the stems by pulling down the stem. Combine the cranberry juice and water in a small saucepan. Add the sugar.

Heat over medium heat, stirring gently to combine. Once the sugar has dissolved, add the rosemary leaves, using a mesh tea ball if you have one, for easier cleanup. The infusion likely needs only 5 minutes with fresh rosemary; you want the herb's flavor to be present but not too floral. Remove the pot from the heat. Strain the syrup, if needed, through a fine-mesh strainer to remove all the leaves.

Bottle in a clean container with a lid, and store in the refrigerator for up to 2 months.

NOTE: Pure cranberry juice has high enough acidity that this syrup can be preserved to be shelf stable through the process of water bath canning at home. See the note on canning on page 29.

65

APPLE BUTTER

Makes about 2 pints

8 apples (about 2½ pounds)

1½ cups water

½ cup (1 stick) butter

½ cup packed brown sugar

1 teaspoon salt

1½ teaspoons ground cinnamon

¼ teaspoon ground ginger

½ teaspoon grated nutmeg

⅛ teaspoon ground cloves

Use in Hot Spiced Cider (page 175), Nonalcoholic Buck (page 167), Apple Betty Martini (page 229), Home for the Holidays on the Ranch (page 235), and Hot Toddy (page 242).

You're right, a fruit butter isn't a syrup, but it's here in this chapter because it's a similarly useful sweet preserve for the home bartender. As with syrups, jams preserve fruit through sugar, but fruit butters and jams contain less water and are cooked down to a further concentration. A tablespoon of jam is an easy substitute for a simple syrup in shaken cocktails (they will not work well in a stirred cocktail, because shaking is needed to break up the jam for a smooth drink).

Most folks know apple butter as a recipe that cooks down apples, sugar, and spices far past the applesauce stage, until the apples have caramelized and cooked out nearly all their water content, so far that they reach a rich, glossy, and spreadable consistency. Much like peanut butter, the recipes for this spread typically contain no butter. Hold your horses, because OUR version does.

Call us crazy, but we submit to you preserves that are creamy and rich, a veritable one-ingredient wunder toast–making machine. We were introduced to using actual butter in apple butter recipes by a friend and staffer at our restaurant, whose recipe our customers frequently comment is the best they've ever had. Her recipe is a passed-down secret, and as the keepers of a few heirloom recipes ourselves, we appreciate the secrecy, so this is our interpretation of her recipe.

Like all apple butters, this is a great way to preserve an abundance of fruit. The best apples to use are sweet to sweet-tart varieties, such as Golden Delicious, Fuji, Jonagold, Pink Lady, or Gala. You can also use soft or imperfect-looking apples, which is great as those tend to be the worst eating apples, and apple butter can help you use them up. This apple butter is used in such cocktails as the Home for the Holidays on the Ranch (To Find Love) (page 235) and also adds silkiness to the Orchardist Liqueur (page 107), but do not miss the chance to slather it on sourdough toast, serve it on a winter cheese board alongside German sausage, sharp Cheddar, blue cheese, and walnuts, or pair it with a sharp, aged white Cheddar for a decadent grilled cheese.

Peel, core, and roughly chop the apples. Place the apples in a Dutch oven or large pot with a lid, add 1 cup of the water, and bring the water to a simmer. Cook, covered, over medium heat until the apples are fork-tender, about 5 minutes. At the same time, brown the butter in a skillet over medium-low heat, keeping the heat low enough to avoid scorching the butter as it cooks, but letting it develop a caramelly color and scent. When the apples are done, drain out any remaining water and mash them with a potato masher, or use a traditional blender or an immersion blender. A masher will produce a chunkier texture, whereas blenders will give a smooth consistency. Add the pureed apples back to the pot along with brown sugar, browned butter, salt, cinnamon, ginger, nutmeg, and cloves, and stir well to coat the apples. Cover partially (let the lid sit ajar) and cook over low heat for another hour and up to 3 hours, stirring occasionally to keep the apples from scorching. You will know the apple butter is done when it is thick and glossy and does not run off the back of a wooden spoon when it is turned upside down. Store in airtight jars with lids and refrigerate for up to 2 weeks.

SHRUBS

Shrubs are a concentrated tart-sweet syrup made by combining sugar and vinegar with fruit, herbs, and/or spices. Sometimes called "drinking vinegars," shrubs are a ferment that trace back to Roman times and were a popular way to preserve fruit in colonial America, prerefrigeration. For modern drinkers, shrubs remain a tasty and handy way to preserve produce so that it can be enjoyed out of season—they store for a year, refrigerated, due to the vinegar's high pH. They are usually combined with still or sparkling water to make healthier sodas that can help aid digestion. In the modern craft cocktail resurgence, they're also beloved for the bright, fruity zing (thanks to that high pH) that they bring to cocktails. Combining the sweet and acidic flavors into one mixer makes it easy to balance cocktails and nonalcoholic drinks, because the complexity our taste buds crave, the push and pull between sweet and sour, is built into a shrub.

The type of vinegar you use for your shrubs will make a difference in flavor, from the sweetness of the vinegar to the acid strength—from a strawberry balsamic to pear-cinnamon apple cider shrubs, the possibilities are endless!

They're also a great way to use less attractive fruit and vegetables, or even scraps. Shrubs love scraps. There is juice, or rind, and therefore flavor, clinging to citrus peels (watch the length of infusion so that these do not make the shrub bitter), cucumber ends, or strawberry greens—use them in these recipes.

Shrubs can be processed cold or hot. We prefer most shrubs to be cold processed, as the vinegar and sugar work together to break down the fruit and extract the flavor gently, rather than speeding the process with heat, which can mute flavors or add cooked ones, such as a jammy, caramelized sugar taste. The disadvantage of cold-process shrubs is that they take longer. The advantage is that they process very easily in a hands-off method, mostly in the fridge in a wide-mouth mason jar, letting the flavor develop day by day for three days to one week, until they reach the flavor you like. If you have the time to wait, a cold-processed shrub is the way to gain purer and fresher tasting flavors from delicate ingredients, such as herbs and berries. However, if you are having people over tomorrow and just can't wait, you may prefer to use the hot process, especially if you are making a shrub with hardier roots and spices, such as cinnamon and ginger, which take longer to infuse at low temperatures.

If you're most interested in the health benefits of drinking vinegars, be sure to purchase a vinegar with the "mother" (such as Bragg Organic Apple Cider Vinegar) and limit heating the vinegar so that the beneficial probiotics are not missed.

69

BASIC SHRUB

Makes about 12 ounces

1 cup organic cane sugar

½ cup fruit, berries, and/
or vegetables, peeled and
roughly chopped

1 cup vinegar, such as cider
vinegar, Champagne vinegar, or
balsamic vinegar

1 tablespoon to ¼ cup aromatics,
such as spices or fresh herbs—use
less for stronger flavors, such as
peppercorns, and more for softer
ingredients with more subtle
flavors, such as mint or sage

COLD-PROCESSED SHRUBS

Combine the sugar and fruit in a bowl or a quart-size wide-mouth mason jar
and stir. Let sit at room temperature for a few hours while the sugar draws
juices from the fruit and dissolves into a syrup.

Next, add the vinegar and spices and/or herbs to the jar. Leave at least an
inch of space at the top. Cap the jar and screw on the lid, but not too tightly—
the shrub may create gases that make it hard to remove, and that's good. The
cold fermentation is part of what makes the shrub's flavor and has great health
benefits. Store the shrub in the fridge, shaking it one or two times a day for
3 to 7 days, or until the desired flavor is reached.

When cold-processing shrubs in a mason jar, do not follow our usual
syrup-making advice about infusing syrups in tea bags (remember, this is so
that you can adjust layered flavors and remove some ingredients at different
times), because there just isn't room in a mason jar. We feel deeply that shrubs
should take minimal effort to prepare and create no mess. So, if I want to dial
back one ingredient but let the others keep marinating and getting stronger, I
will strain out all the ingredients and then just add back to the jar the ones that
have yet to reach their full potential.

When the desired flavor is reached, use a fine-mesh strainer sitting in a
funnel over a second jar or bottle to strain out all solids, then transfer the shrub
to a fresh jar for storage. Discard or compost the flavoring ingredients. Label
the shrub. Shrubs will store in the fridge for up to 1 year!

HOT-PROCESSED SHRUBS

Remove the herb leaves from the stems and roughly chop the fruit or
vegetables—they need not be peeled or diced with precision; just give them a
good cleaning and rough chop. Size and shape of the cutting doesn't matter
because cooking time and texture won't be a factor in a shrub, but you do want
to expose as much of the flesh as possible to allow it to best flavor the shrub.

Gently heat the sugar and vinegar in a saucepot over medium-high heat,
stirring to dissolve the sugar. Once the sugar has dissolved, add your fruit or
vegetables. As they begin to heat and soften, reduce the heat to medium. You
may want to mash the fruit with the back of a wooden spoon to speed the
breakdown process and get the ingredients to release their juices. Over very low
heat, add the spices and/or herbs. Infuse these in order of how long they need
to infuse, using the recommendations in the infusion chart (page 30), tasting as
you go, until the flavor is round and present but not bitter.

Strain the syrup through a fine-mesh strainer to remove all seeds and
other solids. Bottle in a clean container with a lid, and store in the refrigerator
for up to 1 year.

STRAWBERRY, PEPPER, AND MINT SHRUB

Makes about 12 ounces

1 cup granulated cane sugar

½ cup strawberry pieces

1 cup white wine vinegar or cider vinegar

½ cup chopped cucumber

½ cup chopped Anaheim, jalapeño, or serrano peppers (your heat preference), guts and most seeds removed; stems are okay

¼ cup combination of fresh mint and fresh cilantro; whole stems and leaves are fine

Makes a great Shrub Soda (page 164), or serve it with a shot of tequila or vodka and 3 ounces of club soda for a cocktail.

Shrubs are the recycling can of a kitchen. It doesn't sound cute, but we can assure you that these mixers will take your kitchen scraps and make them taste exotic and utterly cool. Here, we're recommending one mixture that we love, but if your own scrap mixture tastes good together in a dish, you can probably put it together and make a good shrub. What makes this one work in particular is the combination of a sweet fruit, green pepper, and herb hitting multiple flavor profiles while complementing one another.

Did you make tacos al pastor with cilantro, pineapple, and lime last night? Add the cilantro stems, pineapple core and peels, and lime peels to a vinegar-sugar bath. The leftovers will emerge a week later, transformed. Belinda typically has a few combinations of shrubs in some stage in her fridge, culled from leftovers. This example uses the same ingredients as a salad that she makes often in summer; the "waste" from the salad—such as the stemmed jalapeño cap and strawberry ends (leaves and all are fine)—go to great use in this shrub!

Combine the sugar and strawberry pieces in a wide-mouth mason jar and stir (or cap with a lid and shake the jar). Let sit at room temperature, covered with a clean towel, for a few hours until the sugar dissolves into a syrup. Then, add the vinegar to your jar; there should still be plenty of headroom to add your flavoring ingredients.

Next, add the cucumber and peppers to the jar. Using ends and scraps is fine! However, remember that the more pepper seeds and veins you leave in the jar, the spicier your shrub will be.

Put the jar in your fridge and shake the jar HARD for about 1 minute daily for 3 days. At this point, remove the peppers and add the herbs, leaving the strawberry and cucumber pieces in the jar. Infuse for 1 more day, or until the preferred flavor is reached, then use a fine-mesh strainer sitting in a funnel over a second jar or bottle to strain out all solids. Transfer the shrub to a clean jar for storage. Discard or compost the flavoring ingredients—they've lived two full lives already. Label the shrub. The shrub will store in the fridge for up to a year.

LEMON
CHAMOMILE
SHRUB

Makes about 12 ounces

Juice of 2 lemons, plus the
whole peels

1 cup granulated cane sugar

1 cup light vinegar, such as white
wine vinegar or Champagne vinegar

½ cup dried chamomile flowers,
or 1 cup fresh (see Note)

Makes a Shrub Soda (page 164)
and Among the Wildflowers
cocktail (page 208), or use for
a highball cocktail with 1 shot
of liquor and 3 to 4 ounces of
club soda.

The lemon is here just to offset the delicate chamomile flavor and cover
some of the astringency of the vinegar. We've found that floral shrubs
made without any other "backdrop" ingredient lose their delicate flavors.
Plus, we always have a lot of citrus peels left over after squeezing fresh
juice for other beverages, such as lemonade or whiskey sours, and we
freeze the peels to use when we need them.

Cold process the shrub by combining the lemon juice and peels with the sugar
in a quart-size mason jar, stir or cap, then shake well. Let sit at room temperature
for a few hours until a syrup forms. Add the vinegar and chamomile to the jar,
cap and shake it vigorously, then store in the fridge and shake the jar a couple of
times per day. Infuse the peels for 2 to 3 days total, refrigerated, before removing
and discarding them. Leave in the chamomile flowers and continue to infuse for
up to 2 weeks to coax out their gentler flavor.

Strain out all seeds, peels, stems, and petals. The seeds of chamomile are
tiny and may pass through a fine-mesh strainer. They are full of flavor and
we leave them in, but if you prefer, you can strain the syrup again through
cheesecloth or a CHEMEX brand or other pour-over glass coffee container
lined with a fine coffee filter.

Bottle in a clean container with a lid, and store in the refrigerator for up
to 1 year.

NOTE: You can make the recipe with fresh chamomile, but you will need a full
cup of flowers to get the same potency. Prepare fresh flowers by removing all
green stems and leaves and leaving the flowers on a countertop for any critters
to disperse. For the best flavor, do not rinse the flowers—this will help keep
their delicate scent compounds intact.

73

CELERY SHRUB

Makes about 12 ounces

1 bunch (about 1 pound) celery, well washed and chopped roughly

½ cup water (optional)

1 cup pure organic cane sugar

Juice of 1 lemon

1 cup distilled white vinegar

Makes a Shrub Soda (page 164) or combine with Veggie Garden Vodka (page 100) or Kale and Chard Vodka (page 101) to make a highball cocktail with 1 shot of liquor and 3 to 4 ounces of club soda.

Celery shrub is a revelation. This shrub tastes how we think celery should always taste but without all that stringy, watery texture of raw celery getting in the way. The cold-processed shrub pulls the pure concentrated flavor from the root vegetable and makes tart-savory celery sodas that are surprisingly delicious.

Puree the celery in a blender with the ½ cup of water, or if you are using a juice extractor, omit the water and juice the celery. If you use a blender, strain out the pulp by placing a fine-mesh strainer over a bowl, add the blended juice to the strainer, and let it drip into the bowl. Next, combine the celery juice, sugar, and lemon juice in a mason jar, cap, and shake vigorously until most of the sugar dissolves. (Alternatively, blend the shrub in your blender to more easily dissolve the sugar, then transfer it to a quart-size mason jar.) Add the vinegar and shake again. Cap the shrub and store in the refrigerator, shaking it every day for the first few days to continue to dissolve the sugar.

Bottle in a clean container with a lid, and store in the refrigerator for up to 1 year.

NOTE: The celery leaves also hold delicious flavor; don't be afraid to add them to the juicer or blender.

NO-WASTE SPICED LIME SHRUB, AKA GINGER SWITCHEL

Makes about 12 ounces

1 cup raw cider vinegar, warm to the touch but not hot

1 cup granulated cane sugar, raw honey, or pure maple syrup

¼ teaspoon fine sea salt

¼ cup grated or roughly chopped fresh ginger, from 1 (4- to 6-inch) length of ginger

1 tablespoon broken cinnamon stick

Two lime peels, juice and pulp still clinging

Makes a Nonalcoholic Buck (page 167) or Buck cocktail (page 183). Also use in the Crown Jewel (page 205).

Another probiotic-friendly drink in the shrub category, switchels are a subcategory that always include freshly grated ginger and a ton of electrolytes. Whereas the Making Hay Shandy (page 187) is what you drink after a long day of making hay, this is what you should drink midevent, to hydrate and replenish electrolytes. Raw honey or pure maple syrup will be the healthiest sweetener to choose, whereas organic cane sugar keeps a strictly ginger flavor that some prefer for their cocktails. You can swap out your bottled "sports drinks" for a switchel, or keep it nonalcoholic or add liquor to make a Buck (pages 167 and 183).

When Venise Googled "most profitable crop to grow on small acreage" in 2013 and began a 10-year journey of growing heirloom garlic, the other plants that came up were ginseng and ginger. Because ginger is a tropical plant, you may not have tried growing it in your garden before, but you can do so successfully in a greenhouse or outside in pots that will insulate and warm the soil.

Ginger beer is a key cocktail mixer and this shrub can be used as an affordable replacement. The shrub's longevity in the fridge means you'll always have some handy when you want to mix up a drink. The recipe's heavy lime addition makes it easier to use in mule recipes; you can even skip the fresh lime.

Every time you make a drink with citrus, save the peel after you juice the fruit in a resealable plastic bag in your freezer and add to it gradually. Then, pull out the bag of frozen peels every time you need to make a new batch of this shrub. So much flavor was being wasted every day before we began making this regularly, and you're going to love the way the zesty lime taste develops hands off, over time, in your fridge! Ginger freezes beautifully as well, so whole roots can be put in the freezer for whenever you feel like mixing up this shrub.

To serve, dilute 1 part shrub to 6 parts water or seltzer, or stir into cocktails.

Combine the warm cider vinegar and the sugar, honey, or maple syrup in a quart-size glass jar and stir. Add the salt, lime peels, ginger, and cinnamon, then seal and shake the jar well to mix. Uncap and cover the jar's opening with a breathable cloth, such as a clean cotton dishcloth or muslin, and leave out on the counter overnight. Then, transfer it to the fridge and continue to cold-infuse the shrub. Let the lime infuse for about 1 week in the fridge before removing the peels and discarding them. Leave in the ginger and cinnamon and continue to infuse for up to 2 weeks, until spicy to your taste.

Then, strain the shrub, seal, and store in the fridge for up to 1 year.

BEET SHRUB

Makes about 12 ounces

1 cup cider vinegar

1 cup brown sugar

2 cups peeled and chopped beets
(see Note)

Makes a Shrub Soda (page 164),
Heart Beet (page 245), or Bull's
Blood & Bourbon (page 247).

Beets can be a hard sell, but we can guarantee this is one of the prettiest mixers you can make with the most intense magenta coloring, so maybe we can hook you with the aesthetics and then trick you into loving this humble root veg? We've surprised many with this shrub, which makes a killer whiskey highball or intense Shrub Soda (page 164) on its own.

This shrub is a great example of the taste differences between hot- and cold-processed shrubs. We never make this as a hot-process shrub; the heat dulls the intense sweetness of the beets and makes it taste more vegetal. You can add spices here if you'd like—cinnamon, clove, and/or star anise all work nicely in moderation—but we love the simplicity of just beets and the molasses in the brown sugar. After all, isn't drinking beets pretty out there already?

Combine the vinegar, brown sugar, and beets in a quart-size mason jar and seal with a lid. Shake strongly for a minute or two, until you can see most of the sugar dissolve. Store in the fridge and shake the jar every few hours the first day, so that the sugar is incorporated or it will harden at the bottom of the jar. Continue to shake the jar once a day for up to 2 weeks, or until it has reached an assertive flavor. Once the desired flavor is achieved, strain out the beet pieces and store the shrub sealed and refrigerated for up to 1 year. Make sure to save those strained beets for garnishes!

NOTE: The beet pieces you strain out of this recipe will double as quick-pickled beets and make an excellent garnish for drinks when speared with a toothpick, so it is worth doing a nice peel and an even, square dice on the beets.

77

ONYX OXYMEL, OR HONEY SHRUB

Makes about 12 ounces

1 cup dried elderberries

1 sprig rosemary

1 teaspoon whole cloves

1 teaspoon grated fresh ginger

1 tablespoon ground turmeric

1 cup cider vinegar, preferably raw and organic

1 cup raw honey

Try the Bonfire cocktail (page 229), or shake 1 ounce of the oxymel with a shot of gin for a two-ingredient variation of Bee's Knees.

An herbal tonic of honey and vinegar is an oxymel. It sounds pretty mystical, but is merely an ancient preserve made with infused herbs in a honey-and-vinegar blend, which would have been taken as medicine. Raw vinegar, raw honey, elderberries, ginger, and turmeric all are said to have a host of immunity-boosting and anti-inflammatory health benefits. When you get into the habit of making this frequently, you may want to vary the herbs and fruits you use. By changing it up, you may experience different benefits, ranging from possibly reducing the severity of colds (ginger and elderberry, as used here) to possibly reducing gastrointestinal distress (rosemary, peppermint). Fire ciders are a version of oxymels with additional, savory flavored immunity-boosting elements, such as garlic and hot peppers, taken daily as a wellness shot. We've left those savory elements out of this recipe to get a lot of the same benefits with a milder-tasting mixture.

Similarly to shrubs, oxymels can be processed warm (recommended only for hardier roots, fruit, and woody herbs) or cold. The powerful antiseptic properties of honey mean that an oxymel can even be shaken and stored, sealed, on a counter at room temperature instead of the fridge, and left to infuse over a period of three to five weeks. However, since this oxymel recipe contains elderberry, and uncooked elderberries are toxic and will cause gastrointestinal distress, it must be processed hot. Cooking the berries makes them safe to digest, whereas dehydrating them alone does not.

Drinking a daily soda of this oxymel is an enjoyable way to get your daily natural medicine boost.

Combine the berries, rosemary, cloves, ginger, turmeric, and ½ cup of the cider vinegar in a saucepan over medium-low heat. Cook slowly and gently for 7 minutes, or until the berries begin to soften and burst, while the herbs and berries flavor the honey, turning it an inky purple. Keep the heat medium-low, as your goal is to gently cook the berries and incorporate the vinegar without allowing it to boil and kill the live cultures (this begins to happen over 125°F). After this stage, the berries should be completely cooked, removing their potential toxins, and the aromatics should be well infused.

Remove the syrup from the heat, and while it is still warm, stir in the honey and the remaining ½ cup of cider vinegar. This will protect the added vinegar from the heat, preserving its acetobacter and lactic acid cultures. Last, strain the syrup to remove the spice and berry pieces, and store the oxymel, sealed and refrigerated, for up to 1 year.

FIG CARDAMOM SHRUB

Makes about 12 ounces

3 to 5 green cardamom pods, cracked open

1 cup whole frozen, fresh, or dried figs

1 cup pure organic cane sugar

½ cup cider vinegar

½ cup balsamic vinegar

Figgy Pudding Fizz (page 245) and "It Was Mutual" Highball (page 248) demand that you make this shrub, but it drinks beautifully in simple Shrub Soda (page 164) as well.

Fresh figs can be harvested for only a few weeks a year. They don't keep, and they don't travel well, so if you're lucky enough to have a fig tree in your yard, the pressure is on to eat all the fruit that fall like tasty little time bombs. When you see them at the store in late summer, grab them. Lucky for you, you can extend that short window to enjoy them fresh by preserving them in a shrub. We kind of love how much of a diva figs are, and drinks do, too—the flavor is distinctive and holds up well to a wide variety of liquors.

This is a shrub we prefer to process hot, as the caramelly flavors with the cooked figs are the end goal. If you're making this outside of fresh fig season, dried figs will also work; when heated with vinegar, they will rehydrate.

Whole cardamom pods may not be in your pantry yet, but they can be found easily and affordably online or on well-stocked grocery store shelves.

Toast the cardamom pods in a pot over medium-low heat, just until pods become fragrant, from 30 seconds to 2 minutes. Then, add the figs, sugar, and both vinegars, stirring to dissolve the sugar and increasing the heat to medium. Once the sugar has dissolved and the figs have softened, you can mash the fruit gently with a wooden spoon and coax them into releasing their juices. Control the heat so the shrub does not reach a boil. Infuse for about 20 minutes, tasting as you go, until the cardamom spice flavor is present without becoming overly bitter.

Strain out the figs and cardamom pods. Bottle in a clean container with a lid, and store in the refrigerator for up to 6 months.

PEPPER HOT SAUCE

Makes about 6 ounces

3 or 4 fresh, small, thin, and mild- to medium-hot chiles, such as Thai or cayenne chiles

6 ounces distilled white vinegar

> Add to mocktails, such as At High Noon (page 171) or cocktails for a savory zap of heat. Use in the Bloody Mary (page 222) or Bloody Bunny (page 201).

This is not a shrub but a flavored vinegar, and another recipe that is so simple it hardly counts. Still, it earns its ink in this book because it will be a heavy hitter in both your home bar and kitchen. We learned this from Heather Earnhardt, a Southern-raised chef whose sauces and condiments are legendary around Seattle, and since making it that first time, Belinda has always kept a jar in the pantry. Pepper hot sauce is just hot chile peppers added to bright, tangy white vinegar to pull out their heat and flavor.

Leaving out the other spices, garlic, salt, or butter that more ornate hot sauce recipes contain, makes this sauce incredibly versatile for use in a variety of drink and food recipes. Use it anywhere a little heat is desired, and the vinegar's tang can mingle easily with other acids, such as freshly squeezed lemon or lime juice. The hotter the chile you choose, the hotter the results, so consider how much heat will add flavor without scorching the palate of the cocktail drinker. We suggest two chiles that measure between 50,000 and 70,000 Scoville units, approximately. You can use this pepper hot sauce liberally, such as in a nonalcoholic chile tincture, to flavor tomato or tomatillo juices, to add warmth to nonalcoholic drinks that will help mimic alcohol's throat-warming sensation, or to cook with.

81

Wash the chiles. You can roughly chop them to get them to infuse faster, or leave whole for presentation. Place the chiles in a clean glass bottle that has a fluid capacity of at least 7 ounces (200 ml). Pour in the vinegar. Cap and store in the pantry and begin using after 5 days. The longer the peppers sit in vinegar, the more flavor the sauce develops. You can keep it going, just topping off the vinegar in the bottle for months before the peppers lose their heat and flavor.

TINCTURES, LIQUEURS, AND INFUSED SPIRITS

Tincture, liqueur, spirit, liquor, and cordials: these words have different definitions across the globe and across different industries, and some may just sound to you like they could be pedaled by a mustachioed man in spectacles standing on a box on a street corner in the olden days, proclaiming the magic of his elixirs and potions.

In fact, they're all a little different and are used by bartenders and herbalists alike to extract flavor and medicinal or cosmetic properties from plants. In cocktails, they can be layered together; each has a different use and represents an opportunity to build multiple flavor layers.

For instance, a cocktail might look like: 1½ ounces liquor/spirit + ½ ounce liqueur + a few drops of either a tincture or a bitter.

You can also add sugar to an infused spirit to make a liqueur, or turn the tincture you made into bitters by adding some bittering agents. For example, strawberry-infused rum becomes strawberry liqueur when sugar is added; pepper tincture could become pepper bitters if bittering agents, such as cinchona bark powder or gentian and coffee beans, are added and steeped.

When making your own liqueurs and infused spirits, use the infusion chart on page 30 for guidance on how to prepare ingredients and how long to steep inclusions. Taste often, and take notes when you remove an ingredient or add a new one to create your own specialized, highly personal recipes. Even after finely straining your finished batch through a CHE-MEX filter, if you have one, some color will remain in your batches, and that's fine. Commercial filtration equipment is more powerful than what we use at home, but that color is really attractive in cocktails.

After making these recipes, be sure to label the bottles well. Once you get a collection going, it's all too easy to accidentally add Jalapeño Tequila (page 96) where you meant to use Buzz Button Gin (page 92).

Keep Your Liquor Cabinet Straight

Liquor/spirits are fermented and distilled alcoholic drinks, possibly flavored but without sugar added, where the alcohol content is fortified through distillation to higher than 20% alcohol by volume (ABV).

Liqueurs are sweetened distilled alcoholic beverages with a lower alcohol content (generally less than 20%) with flavorings and sugar added.

Tinctures are a cocktail ingredient made from spirits and straight infusions of botanical, fruit, or vegetable ingredients, without bittering agents.

Bitters are a cocktail ingredient made from spirits and a mixture of intense flavorings and bittering agents, not meant to be consumed on their own.

BASIC
LIQUEUR

6 ounces Basic Flavored Simple
Syrup (page 48)

6¾ ounces infused spirit

Liqueurs are sweetened, lower-alcohol content spirits and are easily confused with the term "liquor," which usually refers to unsweetened alcoholic spirits. Typically made by macerating fruit, herbs, and spices into liquor and then adding sweetness, liqueurs range from 15 to 30% alcohol by volume (ABV). The amount of sugar included in liqueurs varies as well. The USA, Canada, and European Union all have different laws dictating what comprises a commercial liqueur. Since for our purposes we just want them to taste good and mix well in cocktails, you can use a basic recipe and then tweak it as you go.

When making liqueurs at home, you will mix an infused spirit with simple syrup. We like to infuse the syrup and the spirit separately for practical reasons; you'll have two ingredients you can use independently, or you can combine them to create a liqueur, giving you a lot of versatility for alcoholic and nonalcoholic drink making. Also, infusing each of the components will lead to a more robust flavor. We mix the syrup at 70 to 85 percent volume of the spirit, for a resulting ABV of 24%. You can adjust this to your own tastes and preferences, including how you plan on consuming the liqueur. If it will be chilled and served as is, you may prefer to increase the syrup-to-spirit ratio.

We usually believe in layering lots of flavors, but in the case of liqueurs, we prefer to keep a single note, or at most, use just a couple of flavors. This increases their versatility in cocktail recipes. Because liqueurs are generally used alongside other spirits, this will make them easier to pair in recipes. We find liqueurs are particularly useful for making floral or licorice flavors more palatable to a wider audience, as in Fennelcello (page 109) and Lilac Liqueur (page 106).

Drink liqueurs chilled on their own as an after-dinner drink, mix them into cocktails as a replacement for a base spirit for a lower-alcohol-content drink, or use them alongside base spirits in cocktail recipes to satisfy the "sweet" in the "sweet, bitter, sour, spirit" formula to bring balance to drinks.

85

STORAGE TIP

Anything in your bar cabinet with an ABV percentage of 15% or lower should be kept in the fridge. Because this liqueur recipe has an ABV of 24%, it can be kept at room temperature, but it should still be stored sealed in a cool, dark place, such as a bar cabinet, rather than left out on a bar cart under a window.

Combine the syrup and spirit in a quart-size mason jar and shake well. Either store the liqueur in the jar, sealed, or use a funnel to decant the liqueur into a clean glass bottle that narrows at the neck (e.g., a recycled sauce or liquor bottle) for easier pouring. Make sure to label the liqueur. At this level of ABV, the liqueur can be stored in a cool, dark place (unrefrigerated) for up to 3 months, but it will last longer and stay fresher if sealed and refrigerated.

HERB TINCTURE

Makes about 12 ounces

½ cup dried sage

¼ cup dried thyme

¼ cup green coriander seeds

12 ounces (½ [750 ml] bottle, aka a fifth) 151 overproof rum, such as Wray & Nephew brand

Add any time you want to add a dash of herbal flavor without adding sweetness, especially when fresh herbs are not available. Use for mocktails like the Simple Syrup Soda (page 164) or Bitters & Soda (page 166), or cocktails, such as the Green Goddess (page 206), Pitcher Punch (page 221), or Smash (page 215).

This tincture can be used liberally in any drink where an herbaceous note is needed, without adding sweetness or bothering with a muddler. We make several versions each year, varying which herbs we include, and have even blended a few bottles together when we feel risqué. This recipe is great because it can be made year-round, using dried herbs. It makes lovely Christmas presents that you can start in November when your garden is no longer providing fresh herbs.

It never fails to amaze us how many gardeners grow amazing fresh herbs, but also have dusty old store-bought herbs in their spice cabinet that definitely came with them from the last house or were inherited from a family member. Don't waste your herbs: hang them to dry every season and put them in jars, then use them to make bitters! (See page 122 for herb-drying techniques.)

Using dried herbs for bitters and tinctures is simpler than using fresh, as they will infuse more slowly and consistently, allowing you to make adjustments more easily. You can use fresh herbs, but the infusion times will be much shorter and the aromatic oils in the herb leaves will be stronger and subject to off flavors if left in too long. See the infusion timing guidelines on page 30.

Combine the sage, thyme, and coriander seeds in a wide-mouth jar, then cover with the rum. Push down any bits that stick out of the rum. Cap the jar tightly. Infuse for 2 to 3 weeks in a shaded spot, such as a closet or cabinet. To finish, carefully strain the rum into a bowl, then transfer the bitters to small dropper containers, washed-out vinegar or hot sauce bottles, or other small, narrow glass bottles for easy dispensing into drinks. When stored, sealed, at room temperature, tinctures last for a year or more.

NOTE: High-proof alcohol is very useful to extract flavors fully, but in a pinch, you can make a tincture using vodka or light rum. If you do, let the infusion sit for a few days longer than the recipes suggest, since the infusion time is slower at lower proofs.

STORAGE TIP

Tinctures are high-proof alcohol that can be stored indefinitely, but will keep their flavor best if used within 1 year and stored away from light. Amber-colored glass bottles work best for storing tinctures for this reason.

PEPPER TINCTURE

Makes about 12 ounces

½ cup red Thai chiles, or preferred hot pepper

12 ounces (½ [750 ml bottle]) 151 overproof rum, such as Wray & Nephew

Add anytime you want to add a little spicy heat. Use for mocktails like the Simple Syrup Soda (page 164) or Nonalcoholic Buck (page 167), or cocktails such as the Margarita (page 190), Verde Maria (page 224), or even the Making Hay Shandy (page 187).

Most drinks can be made more interesting with just a few drops of this hot pepper tincture, which brings an unexpected element of heat and warmth to your cocktails. You can include complementary herbs, such as cilantro or sage, round out the spice profile with whole white and black peppercorns, or keep it simple. We often use this as a layering component, so simplicity helps keep this tincture useful in a wide variety of recipes, without introducing competing flavors.

Take care when working with hot peppers—wear gloves and wash your hands after you've touched them. We've wiped our eyes with hot pepper juice on our hands too many times, and that kind of pain will really interrupt a happy hour!

With a gloved hand to protect your skin and eyes, rough chop the peppers, place them in a wide-mouth jar, and cover with the rum. The more seeds included in the tincture, the hotter it will be. To reduce the heat, omit some seeds. Push down any bits that stick out of the rum. Cap the jar tightly. Remove your gloves and wash your hands. Let the tincture sit and infuse for 1 to 2 hours. To finish, carefully strain the rum into a bowl and discard the pepper pieces. Transfer the finished tincture to small dropper containers, washed-out vinegar or hot sauce bottles, or other small, narrow glass bottles for easy dispensing into drinks. Stored, sealed, at room temperature, tinctures last for a year or more.

NOTE: High-proof alcohol is very useful to extract flavors fully, but in a pinch, you can make a tincture using light rum or vodka. If you do, let the infusion sit for a few days longer than the recipes suggest, since infusion time is slower at lower proofs.

STORAGE TIP
Tinctures are high-proof alcohol that can be stored indefinitely, but will keep their flavor best if used within 1 year and stored away from light. Amber-colored glass bottles work best for storing tinctures for this reason.

87

BARKEEP'S CITRUS BITTERS

Makes 25 ounces

2 cinnamon sticks, broken into pieces

1 star anise pod

6 green cardamom pods, crushed to crack open

Peel from ½ grapefruit peel, clinging juice and pulp and all

Peel from 1 orange peel, clinging juice and pulp and all

Peel from 1 lemon peel, clinging juice and pulp and all

12 ounces (½ [750 ml] bottle) 151 overproof rum, such as Wray & Nephew

Use by the drop to complement a wide variety of drinks, from the Nonalcoholic Buck (page 167) Hot Spiced Cider (page 175), or Bitters & Soda (page 166) to cocktails such as the Old-Fashioned (page 188), Walk in the Woods (page 209), or Nancy's Whiskey Sour (page 232).

We hate waste, so in addition to composting for the garden, we make citrus bitters with leftover peels from daily juicing, rounded out by warm spices. Technically, this recipe lies somewhere between a tincture and bitters since the only bittering agents are the citrus peels, but it can still be used in cocktail recipes where bitters are called for to season drinks effectively. Bitters last forever in your bar cabinet, so if you don't use them often, you may consider taking half of the batch and tying a ribbon around the bottle neck for a thoughtful and useful gift.

Combine all the ingredients in a wide-mouth jar. Push down any bits that stick out of the rum. Cap the jar tightly. Infuse for 2 to 3 weeks in a shaded spot, such as a closet or cabinet. To finish, carefully strain the rum into a bowl, then transfer the bitters to small dropper containers, washed-out vinegar or hot sauce bottles, or other small, narrow glass bottles for easy dispensing into drinks. When stored, sealed, at room temperature, bitters last for a year or more.

NOTES: This recipe yields a larger batch since the bitters do not spoil, so it can be used liberally in cocktails and makes great gifts. It takes a while to make, so trust us that this larger batch is worthwhile.

High-proof alcohol is very useful to extract flavors fully. For these bitters, we do not recommend using any lower-proof spirits, but you can use high-proof bourbon or whiskey with good results.

89

STORAGE TIP

Bitters are high-proof alcohol that can be stored indefinitely, but will keep their flavor best if used within 1 year and stored away from light. Amber-colored glass bottles work best for storing bitters for this reason.

COMPOUND GIN

Makes 12 ounces

Base

12 ounces (½ [750 ml] bottle) unflavored vodka

7 grams dried juniper berries

4 grams coriander seeds

Spices

1 gram, total, of some combination of dried spice aromatics, such as spearmint, lemon balm, thyme, tansy, rosemary, fir, spruce, fennel, Thai basil, cilantro, star anise, anise seed, hyssop, nettle, licorice, cinnamon, cardamom, grains of paradise, and angelica

Another 0.1 gram, total, of a mixture of aromatics from these categories:

FLORAL: rose, chamomile, lavender, gorse flowers, yarrow

SWEET: elderflower, apple, clover, blueberry, honeysuckle

CITRUS: lemon peel, grapefruit peel, orange peel

FOR INSTANCE, YOUR FIRST GIN RECIPE MIGHT LOOK LIKE THIS:

7 grams dried juniper berries

4 grams coriander seeds

0.5 gram hyssop

0.5 gram lemon balm

0.05 gram orange peel

0.05 gram lavender

Gin was a rite of passage for us. A growing appreciation for it was a clear signal of our maturation (not to be confused with maceration, which will happen in the following recipe). Two things happened to help us learn to love gin: we stopped drinking it with cheap tonic water, and we discovered nuanced gins in the new American style, which are distilled with a bunch of botanical aromatics that round out the traditional "pine tree" flavor of juniper. No gin can be made without juniper, but with a little help from its friends, we have discovered a deep love of gin, which brings nuance and depth to cocktails.

Gin is made by distilling a neutral spirit with such aromatics as herbs, spices, and citrus. Compound gin is a close approximation you can make at home without actual home distilling by adding infusions of spices and herbs to vodka. Some recipes call for higher-proof spirits to speed the infusion along, but sticking with a basic 90-proof vodka is a good choice for beginners, so you can taste the changes slowly and add or remove aromatics as you wish to create your desired blend. At higher proofs, infusions happen much faster, and it is easy to overpower your gin with one or two strong ingredients. The most common reason for a gin to go cloudy is too much added citrus, which releases oils that will affect the transparency of the gin, so add it with restraint.

This compound gin is heavily influenced by what you might already have growing in a cocktail garden. The recipe is set up as a formula so you can make many different variations based on what you might have growing or that is easily accessible to purchase; you can experiment to find your favorite gin. The total recipe of aromatics should add up to about 12 grams (a little less than ½ ounce; see Note about measuring). Always label your infusions well with the ingredients you used for them, so you can re-create your favorites or avoid the ones you did not like.

First, measure out any spices you wish to use, and then, working with one aromatic at a time, toast them in a clean, dry skillet over low heat for 30 to 60 seconds, or until just fragrant. Next, crack and coarsely grind any whole spices, using a mortar and pestle or, if you need to get out some frustration, by wrapping them in cheesecloth and hitting them lightly with a mallet. Then, place each aromatic ingredient in a small sachet made from a square of cheesecloth, tied tightly closed with cotton string. Leave the strings long so that you can attach each to a strip of paper and label each sachet with its contents. Leaving these label strings out of the infusion will allow you to easily identify each item and remove it as needed from the mixture at different times.

Sub in your compound gin for any of the recipes in this book that call for a botanical gin, such as Bee's Knees (page 192), Elderflower Vesper (page 206), Back Porch Lemonade (page 219), Cucumber Basil Gimlet (page 216), Seattle Sling (page 227), or Harvest Moon Punch (page 240).

Pour the vodka into a wide-mouth glass jar or Pyrex container. A wide surface area will help all the infusion bags stay submerged in the liquid if you're using a more complicated mixture.

First, infuse the juniper berries and coriander seeds in the vodka, sealed, for 24 hours in a cool, dark place. Shake the jar and add the remaining botanicals (we recommend no more than four additional kinds). The remaining components can be infused using the rough timing guidelines on page 30, and your own taste buds. Taste frequently and make notes about the length of time each ingredient is in! As soon as an ingredient tastes assertive but not bitter, remove its infusion bag. Let other sachets remain in the mixture until you can pick them out of the aromatic lineup with a taste.

When the gin has reached your desired flavor, strain it. To strain out the color, if desired, use a CHEMEX filter or gravity strain through another very fine coffee filter over a period of hours, repeating until clarity is reached—this may take several passes. Store, sealed and labeled, in a cool, dry place. Swing-top or corked bottles will do the job best, over the long term, to keep the flavor.

NOTE: The total yield of the recipe is small, so that you can try new combinations without too much worry about the expense of a big batch if it doesn't turn out as you hoped. Not every batch does, though we've rarely made one that is completely undrinkable. The most common problem is an overbearingly strong flavor, in which case you can add a little more vodka to mellow it out and then continue on your way. Given the smaller amount of liquor, we suggest showing restraint and sticking to six ingredients at most, though some commercial gins may have 20-plus aromatics in their recipe. Due to the small yield size—and the way that a single ingredient can quickly overpower the mix if too much is used—you will be measuring very small amounts of aromatics, which will require a scale that measures to the tenth of a gram.

BUZZ BUTTON GIN

Makes about 12 ounces

1 cup fresh buzz buttons

1 tablespoon lemon zest

12 ounces (½ [750 ml] bottle) botanical gin

Use Buzz Button Gin in any of the recipes in this book that call for gin, such as Bee's Knees (page 192), Elderflower Vesper (page 206), Back Porch Lemonade (page 219), Cucumber Basil Gimlet (page 216), Seattle Sling (page 227), or Harvest Moon Punch (page 240). For a more subtle cocktail, you may want to "split the base": use Buzz Button Gin for just half of the called-for amount of gin. Be sure to give people a heads-up about the buzz button's effects before serving!

Buzz buttons, also referred to as both the electric daisy and the toothache plant, are a gimmick that just keeps giving. Used historically in Chinese dentistry, popularized today by bartender Mariena Mercer Boarini in a drink at the Cosmopolitan in Las Vegas, and found stuffed in Venise's cheeks like a hippie's chewing tobacco in late summer, these weird little flowers have a hold on us. They create a sort of popping or buzzing sensation on your taste buds when chewed, numb the lips and tongue, and increase salivation. The effect of it all is quite a surprising trip, and innocently delightful. The effects last just 15 minutes and are purely physical.

The flowers themselves taste green and citrusy, sort of like spinach leaves tossed in lemon juice, so we like to infuse them fresh in vodka or gin and add some citrus zest to enhance their pleasant tart flavor. The properties will transfer into the alcohol (though not as pronounced as when the flowers are chewed fresh), making this the most fun bottle of booze in your liquor closet.

Gin haters (for the record, we are aghast, and hope to convert you) may swap out the gin for vodka, but if you do, add a little more flavor in the form of infusing your vodka with ½ cup of a fresh herb of your choice. Infuse the herb for only 8 hours, then remove it and continue infusing the flowers. If you add just the toothache flowers to plain vodka, the spinach flavor of the toothache plant can be overwhelming.

Place the flowers and lemon zest in a wide-mouth jar, then cover with the gin. Push down any bits that float and stick out of the liquid. Cap the jar tightly. Infuse for 1 week. To finish, carefully strain the spirit into a bowl, then transfer into a spirit bottle or a clean glass jar and label. When stored, sealed, at room temperature, the gin will keep for 3 to 6 months before its flavor fades.

CHERRY WHISKEY AND WHISKEY-SOAKED CHERRIES

Makes about 25 ounces of infused bourbon, plus 1 pint-size jar of cherries

1 pound Bing cherries, stems removed

One 750 ml bottle whiskey (we prefer bourbon over rye)

Use in Midnight at the Movies (page 215) and The Dashing Gentleman (page 218); also try it in Nancy's Whiskey Sour (page 232).

This recipe defines one of our paternal grandfather's favorite sayings: "Work smarter, not harder." He was known for a collection of colorful metaphors and aphorisms that are known in our family as "Grandpa Val-isms." A self-made man who went from high school to building a business as a contractor and then real estate developer, he maintained a rough wit, razor-sharp delivery, and dark humor. While most use language too colorful for this book, some others included "The job isn't done until the job's cleaned up" and "You can't swing a hammer unless you git your ass behind you" (which was a metaphor for approaching a project with good intention, not just construction form). Whether or not a family member agreed with him, or even asked for it, he'd share his wisdom any chance he got.

There is nothing more agreeable than a recipe that gains you both a cocktail garnish and a spirit in one, like this recipe. When you make it, you will end up with both bourbon-soaked cherries for garnishing and snacking (be warned, they pack a boozy punch!), and the bourbon the cherries were soaking in goes back into bottles and labeled, giving you a decadent mixing bourbon for cocktails. We use Bing cherries for the deep red color of the juice.

Using a cherry pitter, or a metal straw pushed through the center of the fruit, remove the cherry pits and dispose of them. Divide the pitted cherries evenly between two wide-mouth mason jars or glass jars with a swing-top lid. Pour in the whiskey to fill to the top, ensuring no cherries are uncovered. Let sit in a cool, dark place for 1 month. Then, strain about half of the whiskey into a measuring glass with a pour spout, leaving enough whiskey in the jar to only just cover the cherries. Use the measuring glass spout to decant the finished cherry whiskey back into the original whiskey bottle. Label and store for 3 to 6 months for best flavor, though it can be used indefinitely.

FOR THE WHISKEY-SOAKED CHERRIES

Add 1 tablespoon of orange zest and 1 cinnamon stick to the jar of cherries, cover, and store in the refrigerator. After 2 to 3 weeks the cherries will be ready to eat. Refrigerated, they will keep for up to 6 months. (Optional: Add the seeds scraped from ¼ quarter vanilla bean, for sweeter cherries.)

JALAPEÑO
TEQUILA

Makes about 12 ounces

2 jalapeños, stemmed and seeded, guts removed, and chopped roughly

12 ounces (½ [750 ml bottle]) tequila

Use this for Verde Maria (page 224), Margarita (page 190), and Cock's Crow (page 228).

As great as a margarita is, a spicy margarita is just better. But this tequila is not limited only to its margarita form: it has lots of potential as a Ranch Water (page 181), a Paloma (see Cock's Crow, page 228), and more. Heat can play an important role in adding an intrigue and mouthfeel to cocktails that make you want to keep sipping. If you grew a spicier pepper than jalapeños and want to try adding them to tequila, make sure you use a little less pepper and be sure to remove all the seeds and veins, as they hold the most heat. Peppers infuse very quickly, so do not leave the spirit too long before tasting it. Spicy food is fun, but when combined with the burn of alcohol in your throat, there can be too much of a good thing, so don't go for contest-level heat here. Take care to wear gloves and wash your hands when preparing this—we've had one too many peppery eyeballs to count. Gloves come in handy to prevent this fate.

Place the jalapeño slices, and as many seeds as desired, in a wide-mouth jar and cover with the tequila. The seeds and veins hold the greatest heat, so leaving them in will make for a hotter spirit. Push down any bits that stick out of the tequila. Cap the jar tightly. Infuse for 1 to 2 hours in a shaded spot, such as a closet or cabinet, and taste often to check for heat. Ideally, the spirit you make will have a balance of the green flavor of the jalapeño flesh and the spicy heat. To finish, carefully strain the tequila into a bowl, then transfer it back into a clean glass jar and label. When stored, sealed, at room temperature, the tequila will keep for 3 to 6 months before the flavor fades.

POBLANO LIQUEUR

Makes 8 ounces

4 ounces poblano juice (from 4 to 6 poblanos) processed in a juicer

1 rounded tablespoon granulated cane sugar

1 sprig cilantro

3 dried small Thai red chiles or serrano peppers, broken into pieces, seeds and stem removed

½ jalapeño, stem and most seeds removed, sliced

4 ounces blanco tequila

Make a simple cocktail by adding club soda and ice, use in the Buck cocktail (page 183) or Verde Maria (page 224), and use to make the best Bloody Mary (page 222).

For bartending, one of Belinda's favorite liqueurs on the market is Ancho Reyes Verde Chile Poblano Liqueur. It adds a savory and spicy note to drink recipes. However, it gets expensive to add a lot of additional bottles to your home bar, and Ancho Reyes isn't available at most grocery stores, so Belinda sought to re-create the best parts of the product with a DIY recipe.

Place the fresh poblano juice in an 8-ounce glass jelly jar. Add the sugar, cilantro, chiles, and ½ jalapeño to the jar. Fill to the top with the tequila. Cap and shake, dissolving the sugar, and allow the mixture to sit and infuse for 1 to 2 hours, until your desired heat is achieved. Then, strain the liqueur into a bowl and remove the seeds, cilantro, and chile pieces. If desired, use a CHEMEX filter or gravity strain through another very fine coffee filter over a period of hours, repeating until clarity of color is reached. Either store the liqueur in the jelly jar, sealed, or use a funnel to decant the liqueur into a clean glass bottle that narrows at the neck (e.g., a recycled sauce or liquor bottle) for easier pouring. Make sure to label the liqueur. At this level of alcohol by volume, the liqueur can be stored in a cool, dark place, unrefrigerated, for up to 3 months, but it will last longer and stay fresher if sealed and refrigerated.

NOTE: Could you start with a jalapeño-infused tequila in this recipe instead of regular tequila? Why, yes, you could, and we're proud of you for asking. The commercial product Ancho Reyes is not very spicy—it has more of the savory green pepper flavor—so Belinda starts this recipe with blanco tequila, but you can dial up the heat by starting from our Jalapeño Tequila (page 96).

99

VEGGIE GARDEN VODKA

Makes about 12 ounces

4 tomatoes, quartered

1 cucumber, skin removed, sliced

3 tomatillos, quartered

4 garlic cloves

1 bunch chives, about 6 stems

1 bunch mixed herbs, such as oregano, cilantro, dill, and thyme

1 jalapeño, stem and seeds removed, sliced (optional)

1 tablespoon black peppercorns

One 750 ml bottle vodka of choice

Use this vodka in the Bloody Mary (page 222) and Michelada (page 224), as well as the Garden Gibson (page 202).

Make this during that time in summer when farmers' markets are overflowing with colorful produce and everything in your garden is ready for harvesting all at once. Use the vegetable list in this recipe as a jumping-off point—feel free to add more of what you have. Just don't miss the fresh herbs, chives, peppercorns, and raw garlic, as they make a big difference here.

Combine all the ingredients in a wide-mouth jar. Gently muddle the herbs into the vodka with a muddler, wooden spoon, or tenderizer. (Do not puree the vodka and ingredients in a blender—the herbs will end up bitter, and you want to infuse this one slowly.) Push down any bits that stick out of the vodka. Cap the jar tightly. Infuse for 1 hour, then remove the jalapeño. Infuse for another 4 hours in a shaded spot, such as a closet or cabinet. Remove the herbs. Cap and continue to infuse the vodka for 24 to 48 more hours. Check the mixture every 12 hours for your preferred flavor. This seems tedious, but you don't want to let the mixture get too hot or the herbs to become acrid, whereas the vegetables can sit longer to develop flavor. To finish, carefully strain the vodka into a bowl, discarding the solids, then transfer it back into the vodka container or a clean glass jar, and label. When stored, sealed, at room temperature, the vodka will keep for 3 to 6 months before the flavor fades.

KALE AND CHARD VODKA

Makes 12 ounces

2 kale leaves, rinsed and torn

2 Swiss chard leaves, rinsed and torn

12 ounces (½ [750 ml bottle]) vodka

Make a simple cocktail by adding a squeeze of lemon, club soda, and ice. This infused vodka is also essential for the Green Goddess (page 206) and can be used in the Garden Gibson (page 202) and Bloody Bunny (page 201).

We hear you when you say, "Why is this necessary?" and "Do greens even WANT to be vodka?!" But we insist, they do, and this spirit is a delight. It's a brilliant green to blue-green color, for one thing, and it is just kind of silly for these superfood leafy greens to be in a spirit, which we love. The hearty fibrousness of kale is the reason we don't love to eat it raw, and this vodka serves up the surprisingly gentle flavors of kale and chard without the excessive chewing required in its raw form.

Not much surprises a person in adulthood, but this vodka can, and that's reason enough for us to make it for our unsuspecting friends.

Combine the kale and chard leaves in a wide-mouth jar and cover with the vodka. Push down any bits that stick out of the vodka. Cap the jar tightly. Infuse for 12 hours in a shaded spot, such as a closet or cabinet. To finish, carefully strain the vodka into a bowl, then transfer it back into the vodka container or a clean glass jar, and label. When stored, sealed, at room temperature, the vodka will keep indefinitely, although after 6 months, the flavor fades.

101

BERRY RUM AND BERRY LIQUEUR

Makes about 12 ounces

1 cup fresh berries, rinsed, stems and greens removed (see Note)

12 ounces (½ [750 ml bottle]) rum or vodka

Use in simple cocktails with club soda, a squeeze of lime, and ice as well as the Pitcher Punch (page 221). Can be used in lieu of fresh berries and the rye whiskey in Smash (page 215).

Our mother was the reigning worst berry picker of the Auburn and Kent Valleys in 1974. She hated riding the bus to pick in the fields on summer mornings, something farm kids did back then to earn school clothes and spending money. The youngest of eight kids, she would watch her siblings fill baskets while she hid in the field, fiddling around all day until she could go home. It must be because we never did this as a forced job, that we now love picking berries each summer. Picking strawberries, raspberries, and blackberries is a favorite family pastime that we've passed on to our kids. The number one tip we have for getting kids to pick berries with you is to let them eat as much as they want, and also to make it a competition to fill their cup first. To make each cup, tie a string to a red Solo cup with two holes punched on either side, creating a cup necklace, so kids can have both hands free while picking and look down into their cup for motivation. You'll go home dusty and happy, laden with berries, and make yourself this recipe!

Fruity rum blends effortlessly in cocktails and tastes so much better made fresh with real ingredients, compared to the commercial brands that use only essences and artificial flavorings.

Place the berries in a wide-mouth jar and cover with the rum. Muddle the berries into the rum with a muddler, wooden spoon, or tenderizer. (Alternatively, you can puree the vodka and berries in a blender, and then do a slow gravity strain through a fine-mesh strainer or a Chemex coffee filter, but this involves more equipment; we like the manual, less messy method.) Push down any bits that stick out of the vodka. Cap the jar tightly. Infuse for about 24 hours in a shaded spot, such as a closet or cabinet. Check the mixture for your preferred flavor every 12 hours. To finish, carefully strain the rum into a bowl, then transfer it back to the rum container or a clean glass jar, and label. When stored, sealed, at room temperature, the rum will keep for 3 to 6 months before the flavor fades.

BERRY LIQUEUR

Combine 1 part berry rum and 1 part berry simple syrup (page 48) in a new jar or bottle, label, and store. This liqueur is sweeter than our base liqueur recipe and is delicious served alone. Due to the lower alcohol by volume (ABV), it should be refrigerated.

NOTE: When you strain out your rum-soaked berries, it would be a shame to toss them. It is worth the effort to remove the greens and stems of the berries before muddling them, so you can puree them into a frozen rum cocktail, drizzle them over ice cream, dehydrate them into a boozy fruit leather, and so on.

ELDERFLOWER (OR LILAC) LIQUEUR

Makes about 12 ounces

6 ounces vodka

6¾ ounces Foraged Elderflower Cordial (page 61) or Lilac Cordial (page 60)

Use in simple cocktails with club soda, a squeeze of lemon, and ice, as well as in Sparkling Rosé Wine Spritzer (page 182), White Sangria (page 194), Lilac and Lead French 75 (page 185), Pitcher Punch (page 221), Elderflower Spritz (page 203), Elderflower Vesper (page 206), and Back Porch Lemonade (page 219).

This liqueur is either your perfect entry into floral cocktails, or the plank you'll walk to drown in them. What we mean is, it gets to you. This floral flavor is so universally delicious to pretty much everyone that the industry-leading brand of elderflower liqueur, St-Germaine, is called "bartender's ketchup," for its ability to marry flavors and for the crutch it can become for recipe creators. It's hard to make a drink with elderflower liqueur in it that tastes bad, so it can get overused on bar menus. Luckily, you don't have that worry at home and can add a little of this to every drink you make!

Combine the vodka and cordial in a quart-size mason jar and shake well. Either store the liqueur in the jar, sealed, or use a funnel to decant the liqueur into a clean glass bottle that narrows at the neck (e.g., a recycled sauce or liquor bottle) for easier pouring, and label the liqueur. At this level of alcohol by volume, the liqueur can be stored in a cool, dark place, unrefrigerated, for up to 3 months, but it will last longer and stay fresher if sealed and refrigerated.

BROWN BUTTER VODKA

Makes about 12 ounces

4 tablespoons (½ stick) butter

12 ounces (½ [750 ml bottle]) vodka

It will be a lovely complement to the fall orchard fruit cocktails, such as Figgy Pudding Fizz (page 245), Pumpkin Spice Espresso Martini (page 237), and Apple Betty Martini (page 229).

If you ever wanted your cocktails to have the sumptuousness of dessert without any sweetness, you need to try making this vodka. Fat washing is a bartending technique that introduces a fat to a spirit so that the silky, rich flavors of fats bind to the harsher qualities of the spirit and mellow them out. It allows you to add flavors from fats to a cocktail without overwhelming a drink and it softens the alcohol's harshness. You can fat wash with just about anything from lard to sesame oil, but should you? Not necessarily. But you SHOULD fat wash with browned butter, an obvious choice to add a nutty depth.

Brown the butter in a skillet over medium-low heat, keeping the heat low enough to avoid scorching the butter as it cooks, but letting it develop a deep caramelly color and scent. Do not let it boil, or it will scorch and turn black quickly. Remove the butter from the heat. Pour the vodka into a wide-mouth jar or sealable storage container. Add the brown butter to the top, then stir it in, or cap and shake it. Now, cover the mixture and freeze it for several hours or overnight. The butter fats will harden and separate from the vodka and can be easily skimmed off. Strain the vodka again through a Chemex or a fine-mesh strainer fitted with cheesecloth, until clear and free of any butter bits.

107

ORCHARDIST LIQUEUR

Makes about 12 ounces

1 ripe pear, cored and diced

12 ounces (½ [750 ml bottle]) vodka

2 to 3 tablespoons Apple Butter (page 66), to taste

This liqueur makes a delicious highball cocktail and is cozy in a warm cup of Hot Spiced Cider (page 175). Use for Apple Betty Martini (page 229).

An accident became a staple recipe the year Belinda added apple butter to a pear-infused vodka instead of a plain bottle of vodka. Pears steeped in vodka are given a layer of warm spices and silkiness from homemade apple butter. Choose fully ripened pears for the best flavor. This liqueur makes a delicious highball cocktail and is cozy in a warm cup of Hot Spiced Cider (page 175).

Place the pear pieces in a wide-mouth jar and fill with vodka. Push down any bits that stick out of the vodka. Cap the jar tightly. Let it sit, checking the mixture after 12 hours and gently pressing on the softened fruit to release juices. Infuse for 4 to 7 days total, tasting every day or so. To finish, carefully strain the vodka into a bowl. Combine the pear vodka and apple butter in a quart-size mason jar and shake well. Either store the liqueur in the jar, sealed, or use a funnel to decant the liqueur into a clean glass bottle that narrows at the neck (e.g., a recycled sauce or liquor bottle) for easier pouring, and label the liqueur. At this level of alcohol by volume, the liqueur can be stored in a cool, dark place, unrefrigerated, for up to 3 months, but it will last longer and stay fresher if sealed and refrigerated.

FENNELCELLO

Makes about 25 ounces

1 fennel head, with
flowers and seeds

½ cup fennel root, rinsed
and chopped

Bright yellow fennel pollen, shaken
from 1 head of flowering fennel

12 ounces (½ [750 ml bottle]) vodka

10 ounces plain simple syrup or
fennel syrup

Combine with vodka and use
in simple cocktails with club
soda and ice. Use in the Plenty
Good recipe (page 236) and
Roman's Empire (page 192).
Can additionally be used with
vodka to "split the base" of drink
recipes that call for aquavit
(a Scandinavian liquor you may
not have in your bar cabinet,
which often uses fennel as
an aromatic).

If you want to renature your lawn as all the cool kids are doing these
days, we have a proposal for you: fennel. We grew it one year in the raised
beds and it got big, and the bees loved the flowers so much that we left
it in until the next year to please them. This was a huge mistake. That
next spring, the fennel began to sprout all over between the graveled rows
of the raised beds, in one of our busiest seasons of our business, when
we were understaffed. Unchecked, a thick and feathery lawn of fennel
developed in a single season. But, rest assured, we are definitely on the
bees' good side now.

So, we did the practical thing, and when life gave us a fennel lawn,
we made Fennelcello. It's a wonderful way to use the fennel after it has
gone to seed, putting energy into the flower and seed-forming rather than
the stalks. If you're a licorice lover, this one's for you. If you're not, like
Belinda, try it anyway and we think you will still love the way using just
a bit of this liqueur in cocktails, such as the Roman's Empire (page 192),
adds a whole lot of intrigue.

Most of our liqueur recipes call specifically for the use of infused
syrups and infused spirits, but this one does not. Fennel is such a strong
flavor that those aren't needed, but are still an option.

Combine the fennel head, root, and pollen a wide-mouth jar and cover with
the vodka. Push down any bits that stick out of the vodka. Cap the jar tightly.
Infuse, checking the mixture for your preferred flavor every 12 hours, but
stopping after 48 hours at most. To finish, carefully strain the vodka into a
bowl. Combine the vodka and the syrup in a quart-size mason jar and shake
well. Either store the liqueur in the jar, sealed, or use a funnel to decant it into a
clean glass bottle that narrows at the neck (e.g., a recycled sauce or liquor bottle)
for easier pouring, and label the liqueur. At this level of alcohol by volume, the
liqueur can be stored in a cool, dark place, unrefrigerated, for up to 3 months,
but it will last longer and stay fresher if sealed and refrigerated.

NOTE: All parts of the flower hold flavor, so unlike the lilac or elderflower
cordial recipes (pages 60 and 61) that call for careful preparation of the flowers,
you can use the entire flower head in this recipe, in any stage. The green seeds
have the strongest licorice flavor, so err on using seeded flowers over fresh
yellow flowers full of pollen if you have heads in several stages of growth. Your
fennel patch may not have fennel flowers, pollen, and seeds at the same time.

JUICES,
TEAS,
AND
DEHYDRATING

This chapter focuses on additional ways to extract flavor from seasonal ingredients and to use them in drinks. Juicing will pull all the liquid from an ingredient and leave behind the pulp, fibers, and peels. The juice must be used fresh, or it must be frozen within 24 hours. Juicing is for instant gratification and packs a concentrated flavor bomb. To get the best flavor, you should juice fruits and vegetables at the peak of their season.

Dehydrating and drying will do just about the opposite, pulling out all moisture to leave behind flavor in the peels, flowers, or leaves that then can be stored at room temperature to be used off season. Removing the water content via dehydrating or drying garden ingredients is a long-game method to preserve their flavors for long-term storage. It takes a while to slowly dehydrate the plants without burning their delicate leaves, but the effort pays off when you can use them all year, steeped in hot water in teas, or used in tincture, shrub, and syrup recipes.

Floral waters (also known as hydrosols) are made by extracting flavorful and aromatic oils from plants through boiling or distillation methods—we've included both ways so you can test your favorite. They are highly concentrated and, like tinctures or bitters, should be used sparingly in recipes: just a couple of drops will do.

Juicing for Cocktail Recipes

A juicer, while usually an ungainly large appliance with a lot of parts to clean, is an essential tool for garden-to-glass drinking. Juicing gets the purest, freshest flavor without the fibrous pulp and imparts both health benefits—such as vitamins and minerals from fruit, veggies, and herbs—and also bright color and silky texture.

As a time-saver or to save your favorite juices for your off-season enjoyment, you can freeze them. An ice cube tray works well to store small amounts of frozen juice for future cocktails.

If you don't have a juicer, you can use a traditional blender to blend an ingredient with a bit of water and then slowly strain out all the pulp. This method will avoid buying an extra appliance, but adds a lot of time and has just as many dishes involved. We both found juicers for free in online marketplaces, and we store them with our canning supplies in the basement.

Essential to remember when juicing: Buy or grow organic fruit—or at least fruit and vegetables that have been minimally treated with chemicals. Otherwise, juicing will put these undesirable things straight into you. For the same reason, wash fruit well before juicing. Once you have your fresh juice, oxidation and separation is normal and expected, but not ideal. Drink up quickly or freeze your fresh juices within 24 hours to prevent this fate for your beautiful juice.

113

FRESH-PRESSED APPLE CIDER

Makes 12½ ounces

1 pound apples, cleaned and in edible shape (some cracks or small or misshapen fruit are fine, but spoiled or moldy fruit that has been left on the ground for days is not)

Use in Hot Spiced Cider (page 175), Apple Betty Martini (page 229), Walk in the Woods (page 209), and Harvest Moon Punch (page 240). It is delicious served cold over ice with a shot of Elderflower Liqueur (page 106) or Brown Butter Vodka (page 107).

At the farm, four heirloom apple trees line the front driveway, a private gravel drive that the elk use as a nightly passageway between sets of woods. The apple trees have been here for many farm owners now, seen many kids pick fruit from its branches as in that old Shel Silverstein story, and thankfully, most of its branches stand above the reach of the elk's snacking abilities. In early years at the farm, an old-fashioned wooden cider press was gifted from another family whose kids had outgrown the tradition of pressing apples each fall. Little did we know how essential this tool would become for fall cocktails, as well as to cement a family tradition.

Now, every year, our kids take turns spinning the hand crank until the bucket full of apple grindings is pressed firmly against the wood slots and the cider begins to flow down the wooden ramp, as the kids lie horizontal in the grass with their mouth open wide for the first taste, or slip a cup at the end of the ramp, bypassing our pitchers. A juicer, while less romantic, does the job just as effectively.

For cider, we like sweet-tart apples, such as Pink Lady, Gravenstein, Jonagold, and Jonathan. If you wash the apples well before juicing, you can drink the cider fresh, or you may be more comfortable pasteurizing your own juice to kill off any possible bacteria from the fruit (this also prolongs the storage life).

Wash the apples well to remove any dirt and waxes or coatings on the skin.

Process the apples in a juicer or press. Pressed cider will have a cloudier appearance, which is normal. It can be fine strained through cheesecloth or muslin if there are bits of pulp.

To drink fresh, consume within 2 to 3 days, or the juice will begin to ferment.

To pasteurize the juice before freezing or drinking, heat it to 165°F, or until simmering, and hold that temperature for 5 minutes without letting the juice boil. If you accidentally boil it, it is not ruined! But avoiding a boil will help maintain a vibrant taste. Let the juice cool before drinking and store it, refrigerated, in a clean bottle with a lid (plastic or glass is fine).

To preserve by freezing: Fill a gallon-size resealable freezer bag with the juice, label and date, and then stack them flat. Always leave 2 inches of headspace when freezing to allow room for the juice to expand as it freezes, or you will end up with busted bags or broken glass!

NOTE: You can use the water bath canning method for longer storage life if the pH of the juice is less than 4.6 (select tart apples with a low pH). You can adjust the pH by adding lemon juice. See the note on canning on page 29.

GREEN JUICE

Makes about 20 ounces

3 cups kale, spinach, or other greens of choice, or a mixture

3 celery ribs, including leaves

1 cucumber, cut lengthwise to fit your juicer

One 1- to 2-inch chunk fresh ginger

Juice of 1 lime, squeezed

1 apple, cored and sliced roughly

Optional immunity boosters: bee pollen, turmeric, and/or ½ jalapeño (stem and most seeds removed)

> Drink fresh or mix it into the nonalcoholic At High Noon refresher (page 171).

You know green juice is good for you to drink, but did you know you could also add it to cocktails? Sure, it's a little bit like throwing salt over your shoulder: it might not help you ward off a hangover, but it certainly can't hurt! Mix this juice into a cocktail by adding a shot of Poblano Liqueur (page 99) or Jalapeño Tequila (page 96).

Whether you drink it on its own for breakfast, or you mix it into our At High Noon zero-proof refresher (page 171), green juice uses a blend of vitamin- and mineral-rich garden ingredients to create a sweet-tart-vegetal balance.

Wash the vegetables well.

Process all the kale, celery, cucumber, and ginger in a juicer. Strain out the seeds and pulp. If you do not have a juicer, you can still make this! Wash everything well, peel the cucumber and ginger, and remove any cucumber seeds before placing in a blender. The consistency will be closer to a smoothie. Press the juice through a sieve or strainer to remove the pulp and get a thinner juice.

To preserve by freezing, freeze quickly after juicing. Use a gallon resealable freezer bag, fill, and then stack flat. Always leave 2 inches of headspace when freezing to allow room for the juice to expand as it freezes, or you will end up with busted bags! Freeze for up to 1 year.

NOTE: Separation and oxidation are normal in fresh juices. Freeze right away to preserve color, or serve fresh immediately for the prettiest juice. If storing in the fridge, consume within 3 days and shake before drinking.

FRESH TOMATO JUICE

Makes about 10 ounces

1 pound tomatoes, cleaned and in edible shape. Some cracks, or small or misshapen fruit are fine, but spoiled or moldy fruit is not.

This fresh tomato juice makes the best Bloody Mary or Virgin Mary. Serve it up with or without the alcohol in the Bloody Mary recipe (page 222), and use it for the Michelada (page 224).

Tomato juice reminds us of our dad, because we found it a gross habit of his to order it, as often as he does . . . UNTIL we juiced our own garden tomatoes. Now, we sort of get it because fresh tomato juice is delicious, but Dad's cans could use a major upgrade. And, obviously, this fresh tomato juice is the essential base for our incredible Bloody Mary (page 222) and Michelada (page 224) recipes, so you will want to make it as soon as tomatoes ripen on the vine.

As different as Tang is from freshly squeezed orange juice, or Spam from a just-out-of-the-oven pork roast, that's how different canned tomato and fresh tomato juice are. We urge you to make it fresh and drink it fresh!

If you want to can your own, it will still taste far and away better than the grocer's, because you will be starting with a fresher product of just-picked tomatoes. There are some scary efficiencies taken with conventional tomato products, such as using lye to peel tomato skins—avoid this by making your own! Writing this, we realize that we should really make a tall glass of this more often for our dad.

Wash the fruit well to remove any dirt and waxes or coatings on the skin.

Process the tomatoes in a juicer. Strain out the seeds and pulp. If you do not have a juicer, you can still make this recipe! Cut the tomatoes into quarters and place them in a saucepan. Heat to a boil over high heat while crushing the tomatoes with a wooden spoon. Let the tomatoes bubble and cook vigorously as you crush them. Reduce the heat to medium and simmer for 5 minutes. Press the juice through a fine-mesh strainer lined with cheesecloth to remove the seeds and pulp.

To drink fresh, consume within 2 to 3 days, or the juice will begin to ferment.

To preserve by freezing (our preference): Use a gallon resealable freezer bag, fill, and then stack flat. Always leave 2 inches of headspace when freezing, to allow room for the juice to expand as it freezes, or you will end up with busted bags!

To pasteurize the juice before drinking, heat it to 180°F or until simmering, and hold that temperature for 10 minutes without letting the juice boil. Not letting the juice boil will help maintain a vibrant taste and appearance. Let cool before drinking, and refrigerate for up to 3 days. If separated, shake the juice before drinking.

NOTE: You can use the water bath canning method for longer storage life if the pH of the juice is less than 4.6. You can adjust the pH by adding lemon juice. See the note on canning on page 29.

BOTANICAL WATERS

Makes about 64 ounces

½ cup fresh herbs and/or edible flowers, washed

64 ounces water

Drink fresh or mix it into the At High Noon refresher (page 171). Want to use it in a cocktail? Try these combinations!

Mint, lemon balm, cucumber, and borage flower water—pair with vodka or gin

Cilantro, nasturtium, and cucumber water—pair with tequila, vodka, or light rum

Corn cob, basil, and diced chile water—pair with tequila, mezcal, or Scotch

Plum, cinnamon, and marigold water—pair with whiskey, vodka, or gin

---

Treat yourself . . . with water? This is the kind of recipe that seems downright frivolous to write, but if it wasn't in here, you might forget to DO it, and that would be a great disservice to your garden-to-glass self. Simple infused waters (different from Distilled Floral Water, page 127, which are distilled flavor extracts, meaning you're pulling out the essences at a high concentration) make hydrating more exciting and will increase your water intake significantly if you get into the regular habit of throwing this easy yet delicious recipe together. I often get requests for cocktail recipes without any carbonation, and these waters are a great way to make a zero-calorie mixer without bubbles.

The most important thing to remember is that infusing garden goods in water gives off a subtle rather than a strong flavor because you are not using other methods of extraction covered in this book, such as heat (as in syrup), acid (as in vinegar-based syrups), alcohol (as in tinctures and spirits), mechanized juicing, hand muddling, or distilling. What we mean is, if you aren't tasting strong, in-your-face flavor, you haven't done it wrong! It's actually lovely on a hot day to not be smacked with flavor, but just to have the flavor sort of whisper across the room at you.

Another important note is to be careful that all parts of what you're infusing in your water are edible. For instance, I once saw a rhubarb leaf in a fancy water dispenser at a large event. While it looked lovely, the leaves of rhubarb are unfortunately mildly toxic to humans, unlike the very edible stalk, so this was a very bad idea for those event guests.

While many have enjoyed citrus- and berry-infused water in a hotel lobby, it is fun to dive in to some more exotic flavor combinations afforded us by the garden. Serve as a nonalcoholic refreshment at a party, paired with pretty ice and a fresh herb or flower garnish, and you're well on your way to being hired to cater a wedding bar. Even better if you simply make a pitcher of these for yourself a couple of times a week to keep cold in the fridge and increase your chances of getting in your eight glasses a day!

Gently wash the herbs and flowers. Place in a pitcher and add the water. Infuse for at least 1 hour and up to 4 hours total, then remove the herbs and flowers before storing the water in a lidded gallon-size container in the refrigerator. Store sealed for best flavor.

119

HANG-DRYING FLOWERS AND HERBS

1 bunch or more each of garden herbs, such as dill, basil, rosemary, oregano, marjoram, lemon balm, sage, thyme, coriander, verbena, lavender

The most common and widespread kitchen crime of all time is to have old, tasteless leaves in your spice cabinet. Grabbing fresh herbs from the garden to cook with is such a lovely habit—and can be so easy—that it can be difficult for gardeners to remember to preserve the fresh herbs for colder months. Drying herbs is the easiest thing to do, and this is the easiest way to do it, so just do it, please!

We recommend hang-drying all delicate herbs, such as mint, basil, oregano, and sage, to best preserve their color and avoid burning them in an electric dehydrator. Room temperature is slower, but will yield the best flavor and keep the plants attractive. Hang-drying herbs is also our favorite way to preserve delicate-leafed tea plants, such as stevia, nettle, lemon balm, mint, lavender, and hyssop.

Prepare the herbs by shaking them to remove insects. Cut off any dirty roots, but you likely don't need to wash them if you grew them without pesticides. Avoid washing the herbs if you can, as washing too harshly can remove the flavors from the leaves and petals and risk bruising them.

DRY USING ONE OF TWO METHODS

1. Space saving: Make small bunches of the herbs, no more than 1 inch in thickness, sorting by type. Place these on a tray or on a cool counter out of direct heat or sunlight for an hour or so, so any garden friends have time to escape. Then, secure the bunches with a bit of string or a rubber band. Next, hang these to dry in a cool, dry place away from direct sunlight, such as a pantry, closet, or a corner of your kitchen, until very dry to the touch. Some leaves may fall as they dry, but it won't be too much of a mess. When dry, remove the leaves from the stems and transfer them to clean, dry glass jars. Label each jar with the herb and date, and store in a cool, dark place.

2. Neater cleanup: Place the herbs in bunches in paper bags, one bag per type of herb. Place the bunches in upside down so that the stems are at the top and easier to grab when it is time to remove them. Put the bags in a cool, dry place away from direct sunlight, such as a pantry, closet, or a counter in your kitchen, until the herbs are very dry to touch. Some leaves may have fallen into the bag as they dry, which will save you on cleaning up, and you can pick through the bags so they aren't wasted. When dry, run your fingers down the length of each stem to remove the leaves. Transfer the leaves to clean, dry glass jars, and label with the herb and date.

NOTE: We don't bother pregrinding our dried herbs. Adding them to recipes is easy: just grind the herbs to the correct quantity for the recipe, using a mortar and pestle, or gently crush them with your fingers.

121

DRYING FLOWERS AND HERBS FOR TEA

Makes about 5 cups dried flowers

8 cups nonsprayed fresh herb or flower buds

Use your dried flowers in Iced Tea (page 170) and Creamy Tea Cobbler (page 173).

You can make fresh teas all spring and summer, but while you're enjoying the warm weather months, we implore you to think of the colder times ahead and dry your flowers. This method is particularly good for preserving a large amount of blooms at a time to be used later in teas and in recipes like our floral rimming sugar (page 148).

As a bonus, pinching the top growth early in the season from many edible flowers will encourage and multiply your blooms, so the garden will quickly replenish itself. Flowers that respond best to pinching include calendula, lavender, chamomile, anise hyssop, marigolds, snapdragons, salvia, and scented geraniums.

This recipe calls for a lot of fresh flowers, because using them in tea will go through your stash fairly quickly, and the work of dehydrating is usually done on large trays with ample capacity to fit flowers. It is the sort of thing that is not worth doing unless you end up with a good haul.

Prepare the flowers by shaking them to remove insects. Do not rinse/wash flowers or you will remove the flavor from the petals and risk damaging them. Set them on a tray or on a cool counter out of direct heat or sunlight for an hour or so, so any garden friends have time to escape.

Gently remove the flower heads from the stems and leaves, trying to keep the heads of more delicate flowers, such as chamomile, intact so they are easier to move and work with. Other flowers with large petals, such as roses, will benefit from removing and separating the petals.

Lay out all flowers, separated by kind, in a single layer on dehydrator trays (this recipe will use two to four trays, depending on your size of dehydrator), trying to prevent the flowers from touching one another. Dehydrate on the lowest setting for 8 hours for an electric model, or if you do not have one, simply lay flowers out on screens (old, clean window screens work beautifully) or mesh trays in a cool, dry, shaded spot with airflow and let the flowers dry naturally over a period of several dry, warm days. Label which kind of flower is which. They need airflow to dry well, but shade will help preserve their color, which will fade in direct sunlight.

Some flowers, such as calendula or bachelor's buttons, have brilliantly colored petals when dry but the centers dry brown and are tasteless, so at this point, you will remove the petals from the centers.

After the flowers have dried completely, store them in a sealed glass jar in a dark pantry and use for brewing teas.

NOTE: This recipe specifically references flowers because it uses an electric dehydrator and we prefer to hang-dry most delicate leaf herbs, such as mint, stevia, and lemon balm. Our favorite flowers to dry for tea include chamomile, calendula, rose, lavender, echinacea, anise hyssop, and dianthus.

FLORAL TEA BLEND (NON-CAFFEINATED)

Makes 4 servings

¼ cup dried herbs and flowers (see page 122); our favorite tea blend is a mix of chamomile, echinacea, calendula, and mint

8 ounces hot, but not boiling, filtered water

½ ounce Lavender Honey Syrup (page 57)

Use your tea blends in Iced Tea (page 170) and Creamy Tea Cobbler (page 173).

Blending dried herbs and flowers for tea allows you to play with both flavors and natural benefits of the herbs. For instance, this blend is one Belinda enjoys before bed, because the herbs are said to have benefits ranging from calming and aiding digestion, to reducing inflammation and boosting immunity. There's a corner of Belinda's living room set with a thrifted couch, warm blankets, records, and a reading lamp. It took 35 years for Belinda to find her indoorsy side and her tea appreciating side, but this reading nook and this particular cup of tea allows her to sit still indoors when the weather won't cooperate for anything else. The spot is cozy, the tea tastes good, and the honey—you need the honey syrup, because tea is good but honey-sweetened tea is a whole lot better. This spot and this ritual make Belinda go to sleep at a decent hour, instead of watching TV or mindlessly scrolling her phone for hours until her eyeballs burst, and at the age of 36, getting a lot of sleep is something people tell you is important. We recommend it all: the tea, the honey, the sleep.

Combine your preference blend in a mesh tea strainer. Set the tea strainer in a wide-mouth mug and fill it with the hot water. Steep for 5 minutes, or to your taste preference. Serve with Lavender Honey Syrup.

125

STONE FRUIT TEA

Serves 2

12 ounces black or herbal tea

3 stone fruit, such as peaches, nectarines, or plums, washed, peels left on, split in half to remove the pits, then chopped roughly

Optional additional flavors: 3 or 4 fresh mint leaves or thyme sprigs

Use in White Sangria (page 194). You can also use this tea in Iced Tea (page 170) and Creamy Tea Cobbler (page 173).

Both delicious and impressive, this tea is special enough to serve on its own for a summer cookout or picnic, or is a brilliant base for a White Sangria (page 194) or a whiskey cocktail. No extra sugar necessary for this tea—it is naturally sweetened from the peach infusion.

After they've done their job and infused the tea to your desired flavor strength, remove the peaches but don't discard them! Give the "spent" peaches a new life by infusing them in an overproof rum—there's likely a lot of life left in the fruit and it can make a delicious tincture (see page 86 for tips), because alcohol is a stronger solvent than the tea (high-proof alcohol is more effective than water at pulling flavor).

Brew the black tea to your preferred strength. Add the chopped peaches and herb leaves (if using) to the hot tea. Let the tea infuse while cooling to room temperature for 2 hours (letting tea cool at room temperature is important to prevent clouding). Taste for strength of flavor before refrigerating. Remove the peaches and pulp by running the finished tea through a fine-mesh strainer.

SUN TEA

Makes 4 servings

1 cup fresh mint leaves

½ cup other fresh herbs, such as chamomile blossoms

32 ounces filtered water

Use in Iced Tea (page 170) and Creamy Tea Cobbler (page 173).

Calming, caffeine-free, and an aid to your digestive system, this tea is our favorite herbal tea to keep in the fridge in the summertime to serve iced, and it makes a flavorful, noneffervescent mixer to use in nonalcoholic cocktails. Sun tea is a very specific method of letting delicately flavored teas infuse with only warm instead of high heat, which will help develop more nuanced flavors and keep bitterness levels low.

Prepare the herbs by shaking them to remove insects. Cut off any dirty roots, but you likely don't need to wash them if you grew them without pesticides. Avoid washing them if you can, as washing too harshly can remove the flavors from the leaves and petals and risk bruising them.

Clap the mint together in your hands to release the fragrant oils. Place the mint and other herbs in a jar or pitcher with a lid and top with the filtered water. Seal the lid and let sit in a sunny place for 12 to 24 hours, until steeped. Strain and serve cold.

DISTILLED
FLORAL WATER

Makes about 1½ cups rose water

2 cups fresh rose petals

2 cups distilled water

¾ tablespoon vodka

Use to elevate nonalcoholic drinks, such as Fresh Lemonade by the Pitcher (page 168), At High Noon (page 171), Strawberries and Cream Soda (page 163), Cordial Spritz (page 169), and Creamy Tea Cobbler (page 173). You can also use it in cocktails, such as Nancy's Whiskey Sour (page 232), to add a light floral note.

Distilling your own floral waters is a rabbit hole that may end with the purchase of home-distilling equipment. But trust us, it's a risk you should take—start with these simple DIY versions and see where it takes you! Floral waters extract the beneficial oils from the flowers for multiple edible and skincare uses. For instance, roses are known for anti-inflammatory, antiseptic, antiaging, and calming uses. In drinks, rose water adds a delicate, elegant note, and is completely nonalcoholic, making floral waters a useful tool in zero-proof cocktails.

Making rose water at home takes us back to one of our very first entrepreneurial pursuits: at age seven, making homemade perfumes by obliterating flower petals with a mortar and pestle, then packaging them in antique bottles we found in our stepmom's bathroom and selling them at the end of the driveway. It's a sweetly scented childhood memory and it's funny to think that we really have not strayed too far since then in our pursuits.

Choose only organically grown flower petals not treated with chemicals to make any floral water. The more fragrant the rose, the stronger the rose water, so choose a highly scented variety. Harvesting properly will also lead to stronger rose water, so for best results, pick the flowers in the early budding stage and in the morning when their scent is strongest. You can use any color, though darker roses will leech their color and make a pretty colored rose water.

There are two methods to make rose water at home. One is to use a pot, fitted with a glass bowl, to steam extract the flowers via home distillation. The easier way is more similar to preparing tea. It captures the fragrant oils in the water by extracting them through gentle heat, with a couple of steps to help concentrate the results as much as possible. This method is less precise but far easier to execute for a beginner, so we recommend you start there.

Removing the sepals, the white tips at the end of the petal, will give a sweeter end result. If you're substituting dried petals for fresh, only 1 cup of rose petals are needed.

You may also try the same method with other fragrant, organic, edible flowers, such as lilacs or lavender.

127

RECIPE
CONTINUES

SIMMER METHOD

Prepare the rose petals by lightly rinsing them to remove bugs or visible dirt, but do not submerge or rub the petals, as the aromatic oils will be removed. Next, clip off the sepals, the bitter green or white inner tips of the petals. To make this process speedier, stack a dozen or so petals together before snipping the ends. Repeat until all the petal tips have been removed. Place the petals in a saucepan with the distilled water and weigh down the petals, making them sink into the water and preventing them from floating on top, by using a glass bowl that is just a bit smaller than the circumference of the pot. Cover. Bring to a gentle simmer over medium heat and cook for about 4 minutes, or until roses begin to wilt and release their color, but before the color darkens or browns.

Turn off the heat and put the pot in a shallow container filled with ice water. Let the pot rest in the ice bath, covered, for 1 hour. This will help cool it gently, preventing the rose water from releasing the steam that carries with it the fragrant rose oils. Strain out the rose petals after 1 hour, gently pressing on the petals with a spoon as you go to help release the water they hold. Add the vodka to the rose water to help extend its shelf life. Store the strained rose water in a mason jar or dark amber bottles with droppers (these will work best and make it easy to use in recipes) in the fridge. Rose water made in this method will last 1 month or more, refrigerated.

HOME DISTILLATION METHOD

Prepare the rose petals by lightly rinsing them to remove bugs or visible dirt, but do not submerge or rub the petals, as the aromatic oils will be removed. Next, clip off the sepals, the bitter green or white inner tips of the petals. To make this process speedier, stack a dozen or so petals together before snipping the ends. Repeat until all the petal tips have been removed.

Place a small, heatproof bowl in the center of a medium Dutch oven or pot with a lid. Add the rose petals and distilled water to the outer pot, leaving the inside of the small bowl empty. Place the pot's lid, upside down, on top of the Dutch oven and then, over medium heat, bring the water to a boil. Once you can hear the water boiling, lower the heat and simmer. Add a handful of ice cubes to the outer top of the inverted lid to encourage condensation of the evaporated rose water in the bowl below. As the ice melts, pour off the water and add more ice. Continue this process for about 30 minutes. Then, carefully remove the lid, taking care not to drip any water inside the interior bowl. The petals around the bowl's edge will be discolored and wilted, and the rose water will have collected in the small bowl. Store the strained rose water in a mason jar or dark amber bottles with droppers (these will work best and make it easy to use in recipes). Rose water made in this method yields less, but will not need to be refrigerated and will last up to 6 months.

GARNISHES

Basics of Garnishes

Garnishing a glass is like plating in a competition cooking show—it can get pretty intense and very creative. The social media world especially has exploded the use of over-the-top garnishes that entice a drinker to stop scrolling and order (many of which are very artistic but make very little sense to be in a glass, or would be incredibly interruptive while trying to drink). If you're new to making drinks, I recommend that you walk before you run and keep garnishing simple, and even if you're not new to it, we truly don't believe that God created a more perfect garnish than the humble fresh herb, flower, or slice of fruit.

A garnish isn't just something pretty in the glass, though a fresh herb is certainly going to look lovely floating in one. Beyond looks, a garnish should be a component with functionality. It should give you a clue about the drink you're about to enjoy and invite you in with its color, texture, and scent. A strawberry garnish in a savory tomato-flavored cocktail just doesn't make sense, and it can throw off the flavor of the cocktail if the drinker eats the sweet, fresh strawberry before taking their first sip.

Fresh garnishes are our favorite for this reason. The strong smell of fresh herbs or a ripe berry can hide the smell of alcohol and make you feel that you were just in a garden, no matter where you actually are. Garnishing is one of those things that may seem straightforward to a bartender, until they teach a few cocktail classes and realize that it actually isn't at all, with no two glasses looking the same. To keep the glass attractive, there are some general rules in garnishing that bartenders follow.

Edible only: Choose only edible garnishes for a glass. If it is on a plate, you should be able to eat it, and the same is true of drinks. The most common issue is using nonorganic flowers or herbs in drinks, or nonedible flowers. Many flowers and some herbs are grown to be ornamental and, as such, are sprayed with chemicals that are not approved for human consumption, which is why you can't just go to the hardware store, buy a potted flower, and stick it in your drink (it could be dangerous to consume). If you're really intent on using a cherry blossom branch as a garnish, use a clip to attach it to the outer side of the glass, or rest it on a saucer.

A little prep is required: Prewash any fresh produce garnishes. Cut herbs to size and strip their leaves: herbs should be trimmed so they either fit well horizontally laid flat against the opposite edge of the glass rim or so that when a sprig stands vertically, stem down, the leaves stick an inch or two out of the glass. Stripping the bottom leaves will help keep the herb from affecting the flavor of the drink too much, and it looks much neater in translucent cocktails. This is especially important for such herbs as hyssop and lavender, whose small buds can fall into the drink if submerged, and end up making it messy or clogging your straw. For such herbs as mint and rosemary that have several leaves on each stem, pull the leaves off the bottom half or the part of the stem that is submerged.

Mint looks best in thick bunches, tiki style, placed to one far edge of the glass so you can still lift it to drink and get a whiff of mint without the leaves poking and tickling your face. Alternatively, a nicely shaped leaf looks pretty as a horizontal float. Sage, thyme, and lavender look best standing vertically like a flag, stem side down, in the glass.

Keep it drinkable: Keep garnishes to a limited portion of the glass; you shouldn't have to remove it to take a drink. This is especially true of such garnishes as dusted sugar or cocoa powder, or garnishing with petals, such as crushed rose petals, on top of a drink. Any drinks with floating garnishes should get a straw so you can avoid the embarrassment of getting an errant flower petal stuck to your upper lip or mustache during dinner.

Rim halfway around: Bartenders tend to rim only halfway around a glass, or use a pattern for their rimming salt or sugar, such as a painted stripe or a half-crescent. This allows the imbiber to take a break from the added flavor and texture of salts or sugars.

Get artsy: To add flair, consider layers for the garnish. Just as in a flower arrangement, the varied heights and colors of garnishes in a glass look pretty. The easiest is a tall herb sprig standing in a glass, with something in a contrasting color, such as a berry or flower, floating horizontally next to the tall piece. Easy, but fancy!

133

FANCY ICE

Herbs, fruit, or colorfast
edible flowers

Distilled water

Use to elevate any of the
nonalcoholic drinks found on
pages 160 to 177, or the cocktails
found on pages 178 to 248,
especially the Green Goddess
(page 206) and Clarified Milk
Punch (page 197).

Ice is an ingredient that is as important, or perhaps more, than any other ingredient in the cocktail. Bartenders hand crack their ice, smack it with mallets to make crushed ice, use different-sized cubes for different cocktails to speed or slow the dilution level while you're drinking it, and more than anything, they obsess over clarity. Crystal-clear ice depends on both the filtration of the water used to make it and the speed at which it freezes. (If you want to try, you can make good-clarity ice at home by using ice trays packed inside a small insulated cooler, which is then placed inside a chest freezer.) However, while it looks pretty, the clarity of ice is not actually going to affect the way a cocktail tastes, unless your ice is very old and smells musty.

For the purposes of this book, we will focus less on clarity and more on using enough ice to gain the dilution desired and using the correct shape. Because presentation matters, we'll also focus on fanciness.

Hardy herbs, colorfast edible flowers (meaning they are safe to have inside your drink and they won't lose their color or turn brown in extreme temperature changes, such as freezing), fresh fruit, and many vegetables all make beautiful ice inclusions. See page 35 for which colorfast edible flowers to use for best results in ice.

Over the years, we've learned that to get the prettiest ice, don't just freeze a single element in the cube. A few contrasting colors, shapes, and sizes in the ice, such as three cranberries and two tiny sprigs of rosemary, adds a lot more visual interest than will a single raspberry. For the very fanciest ice, we remove flower petals and use them like sprinkles in the ice, for a variety of color and texture that is spread throughout the cube. A few different varieties of florals with small petals, such as the buds of hyssop, bachelor's buttons, and lavender, are a good example.

135

Wash and prep your botanical or fruit inclusions, removing the stems, trimming to size, and slicing fruits if applicable. Fill ice molds or basic ice cube trays half full with distilled water and add your inclusions, then freeze. Once the first layer is frozen and the inclusion is trapped somewhere around the middle of the cube, fill the tray the rest of the way to the top with distilled water and freeze again. This trick will help to keep the fancy inclusions encased in the ice, instead of their floating to the top or sinking to the bottom of the trays, where they will stick out of the ice and then quickly melt into the drink. To store the ice, remove it from the tray and store in a sealed container or plastic bag so that it retains a neutral flavor in your freezer.

CANDIED CITRUS PEELS

Makes about 12 garnishes

1 large navel orange

2 cups plus 2 tablespoons granulated sugar

1½ cups water (for candying)

Add to Cordial Spritz (page 169), Hot Spiced Cider (page 175), or other sweet nonalcoholic drinks as a garnish; also use for the Cock's Crow (page 228), Crown Jewel (page 205), and Seattle Sling (page 227).

An old-school preserving recipe you don't see as often these days, candied citrus peels are a great no-waste garnish when making cocktails that call for orange juice. They fit well into our "whole animal" challenge of bartending, where you use as much of the product as possible in drinks to reduce kitchen waste. The process of blanching can be tedious and time consuming, but as the saying goes, you can have fast, awesome, or cheap, but never all three. Do this while you're also doing another task in the kitchen.

Don't toss out the syrup you use to candy them in, either! Use the syrup from the candying process to mix in an Old-Fashioned (page 188). After all that blanching, you deserve one.

Prepare the orange by washing the rind with warm water to remove the wax. Next, use a sharp knife to remove just the very top and bottom of the orange and discard these (or save to make a shrub later). Slice the orange in half. Place the tip of your knife just between the orange's flesh and skin to begin peeling it back, trying to peel off the skin (with white pith attached) in one piece. (If your orange is very hard to peel, you may need to slice the orange again and try doing this in quarters.) Set the orange flesh aside (juice it later for the Homecoming Margarita, page 231, or White Sangria, page 194). Now, slice the peel vertically into ¼-inch-wide strips. Bring water to a boil in a saucepan and add the peels to soften them and remove bitterness. Blanch them for 10 minutes, then drain and repeat the process again. Oranges need only one or two blanches typically, whereas lemons or limes will need two to three blanches to remove the bitterness. Discard the water.

To candy the peels, bring the 2 cups of sugar and 1½ cups of water to a simmer over medium heat. Stir gently to dissolve the sugar. Add the peels, lower the heat to low, and simmer until very soft, about 40 minutes.

When the peels are very soft, remove them from the heat and let them drain on a tray lined with parchment paper. Dust with the 2 remaining tablespoons of sugar for extra crunch.

CITRUS WHEELS

Makes about 20 garnishes

4 limes and lemons, or 3 oranges, or a combination

> Without any scent and little flavor to impart in a drink, these can be used liberally, almost universally, as a garnish. They are especially nice to use in hot drinks, such as Hot Spiced Cider (page 175) and Hot Toddy (page 242).

When you buy as much citrus as we do, eventually a lime or two gets shoved to the back of the produce drawer and forgotten, until it no longer looks great for juicing or much of anything. But waste not: dehydrate them! The dehydrated wheels add color and texture without adding a lot of juice or flavor, making them an optimal choice for drink garnishing—plus, they look good.

We especially love to use them to decorate Fancy Ice (page 135), because they will not add color or flavor to an already complete and perfectly balanced cocktail once the ice melts, as fresh fruit frozen into ice will. The fruited ice trend is huge on social media, but bartenders would never use it, for good reason. Garnishes that melt and change the drink's makeup are like uninvited guests, interruptive and distracting.

These citrus wheels are popular for Christmas crafting and are the easiest garnish to reach for in winter. Make a small batch regularly to always have on hand!

A dehydrator makes these easy, but if you don't have one, you can do these in your oven set to low heat for a long period of time. Pick a day when you're home anyway.

OVEN INSTRUCTIONS

Slice the fruit thinly and evenly to ¼ inch thick. A consistent, thin slice is important so that the liquid can be drawn out of the slices evenly on the tray. If the slices are too thick, the process will take forever, and if there is inconsistent cutting/varying slice thickness, some slices will be perfectly dry while others are still mushy.

Arrange the slices on a piece of parchment paper over a wire cooling rack, with ½ inch of space between the slices. Bake at your oven's lowest temperature, preferably 175°F or lower, for 4 to 5 hours. Flip all the slices every hour for the most even dehydration. Be patient, because they must be completely dried out or they will mold when stored. You will know they are done when the color has changed, the flesh has shriveled, and you don't feel any moisture when you press the slices.

DEHYDRATOR INSTRUCTIONS

Arrange the slices on a piece of parchment paper over the dehydrator trays, with ½ inch of space between the slices. Dehydrate at 130°F for about 10 hours, flipping every few hours. Check after 8 hours, because smaller fruit slices may be done, but it may take up to 12 hours for all to finish drying. Again, ensure they are completely dry, and be patient to avoid future molding.

138

CHIVE FLOWER BRAIDS

Makes 4

12 chives: look for chive stems 8 to 12 inches high, and if flowering, select 4 chive stems with flowers

Use only to garnish savory drinks, as the aroma of the chives will interrupt other cocktails. These are perfect for such cocktails as the Bloody Mary (page 222), Verde Maria (page 224), or Michelada (page 224).

One of those totally unnecessary but cute garnishes, this is therefore our favorite. We love how these braids are unapologetically feminine. Herb flower braids remind us of the hours Belinda spent on sports fields, ignoring the balls coming her way while making daisy chains, or the hours Venise spent braiding horse manes in childhood.

Use them to adorn the glass of a savory cocktail. If you're braiding chive flowers, a purple flower puff should stick out of the glass enough that the small flowers won't brush off and get into the drink, while still adding color and scent.

If assembling these ahead of time, put the stem ends in a couple of inches of water, to keep them fresh before using. To use in a drink, hold the braid on one side of the glass while adding ice, so that it will stand up on one side of the glass, lodged in place by ice.

Arrange three stems in parallel in front of you on a table, and if available, place one with the chive blossom in the center, with the blossom at the top farthest from your hands. To make it easier, put a piece of tape across the stems just under the blossom to keep them still on the table while you braid. Leave an inch or so at the tape end unbraided. Then, plait the stems by picking up the right stem and moving it over the center blossom stem, then move the left stem over the center stem. Do not braid too tightly, or the stems will want to splinter and break. Repeat, alternating sides, until you reach the bottom of the stems. If you braid the stems tightly enough, you will not need to secure the end, because the top half that will be visible out of the glass will hold the plaits, though the bottom inch or so may begin to unravel a bit. It will be hidden in ice, so that's okay! Alternatively, you can use the stems to tie a knot or two, but be gentle so you do not rip the herb stem. Repeat until you have completed four braided stems.

139

BLOODY MARY SKEWERS

Makes 4 garnish skewers

8 pickled veggies—choose
your favorites from the Quick
Refrigerator Pickles (page 150)

4 garlic- or cheese-stuffed olives

4 rolled or cubed pieces salami

4 cubed pieces hard cheese

Use as a cocktail hour snack,
as well as a garnish for
savory drinks, such as the
Bloody Mary (page 222) and
Michelada (page 224).

Prepare a tray full of these ahead of time and place them, covered with plastic wrap or stored in a storage container, in the fridge before a party. Whether or not you're serving Bloody Marys (page 222), these skewers are always a welcome cocktail hour snack to put out or serve alongside drinks. Choose hard, noncrumbly cheeses, such as pepper Jack or Cheddar to make skewering easy, and either roll thin, precut salami slices and spear them horizontally, holding the rolled meat in place, or cut a log of salami into 1-inch cubes.

Drain the pickled veggies and olives well. Spear one pickled veggie, one stuffed olive, one piece salami, one cube of cheese, and another pickled veggie on a long bar toothpick, alternating them. Repeat to fill three more skewers. Refrigerate until ready to serve.

140

HERB
BOQUETS

Makes 4

12 medium fresh sage leaves

4 rosemary sprigs, each cut to a
4-inch length

8 thyme sprigs, each cut to a
4-inch length

Use these to adorn cocktails
with herbal flavors, such
as Shoalwater Sea Breeze
(page 244) or Seattle Sling
(page 227).

Little herb presents wrapped in twine are too tedious for us to make for our bar, but are the perfect addition to make at-home drinks look extra special. The general rule of bartending is that anything in a glass should be edible for guests, but no one ever goes around munching on whole twigs of rosemary anyway, so adding a little string shouldn't confuse any of your guests, should it? A bouquet adds color, texture, and scent to a cocktail, alerting the drinker to what they're about to enjoy. Use these to adorn any and all drinks that have an herbal component.

To keep these cute and festive and not entirely interruptive, cut the herb sprigs very small, and limit the bouquet size to a height of about 2½ inches, so it can nestle to one side of the glass and the drinker can still enjoy their cocktail easily.

Have ready four 4-inch lengths of kitchen twine or string.

Wash the herbs thoroughly in water and dry gently on clean towels. When dry, fan three sage leaves so the tips of the leaves point up and the stems are together, pinched between the fingers of your nondominant hand. Layer a rosemary sprig over the middle sage leaf and add a thyme sprig to each side of the rosemary. Pinch the bundle of herbs at the very top of the sage leaf's stem, and strip off the leaves of the rosemary and thyme below that point, about the last inch. With your dominant hand, loop the string around this point and pinch it tight to keep it together while laying the bundle on a flat surface so you can tie a knot. Hold the tension around the string as you tie a bow or knot to secure the bouquet. Place the herbs upright in a shallow amount of water so that just the tips of the stems stay hydrated. This will keep them looking fresh for days.

141

MOJITO
BERRIES

Firm berries, enough for 2 to
3 berries per bar skewer or
toothpick, depending on size
of berries

½ cup rum

¼ cup freshly squeezed lime juice

½ cup granulated sugar

Use for Marionberry Mojito
(page 210) and Southside
(page 213), or any recipe you
make with Blackberry and Mint
Syrup (page 51).

These sugar-encrusted, rum-soaked berries may not be worth the extra dishes every time you make a Mojito, but they add significantly to a cocktail's presentation when you want to make the effort. Even better, you can make a bowl of these and set them out during happy hour as a boozy snack. We love a snack and drink combo!

Prepare the berries by gently washing them and then patting them dry. Skewer the berries cleanly through the center of each berry on bar skewers or toothpicks. Firm berries work best for this recipe, as you will be adding moisture and you don't want them to fall apart. Combine the rum and lime juice in a small, shallow bowl. Pour the sugar into a second small, shallow bowl or saucer. Dip the berries in the rum and lime mixture, rolling them so the mixture coats them evenly; let soak for 1 minute. Then, lift them out and shake gently to get drops off the berries before coating them in the sugar. Rolling them in the sugar will give you a thicker coating of sugar, which is delicious but less pretty. Pinching sugar and sprinkling it over the berries as you rotate them will give you a more delicate coating.

RIMMING SALTS AND SUGARS

Each of these recipes takes some time to infuse the salt or sugar or dehydrate the ingredients, but once you've done that, the recipes are supersimple: just combine one part flavoring ingredient with four parts of salt or sugar, then store them in a dry spot for delicious, colorful, and textured rims for your cocktails. We beg of you, don't stop there. In fact, just go ahead and store these in your pantry, not your bar, so you will remember to sprinkle them on baked goods—use Vanilla Sugar (page 149) to top muffins or Floral Sugar (page 148) to top shortbread—or savory dishes (try fennel salt on risotto and spicy salt on avocado toast).

Don't let salt and sugar blends get wet, or they will clump and be ruined. Pour onto a shallow plate just the amount you need to rim the glass for your cocktail, and store the rest in a sealed jar.

When you're adding decorative and flavored rims to a drink, remember to give people a break. We don't rim the whole glass; we only do halfway around the edge to make a half-moon shape along the rim. This allows people to take a break from the salt or sugar rim when they want to, or ignore it completely. To get sugars and salts to stick to the glass rim, run a wedge of citrus halfway around the rim and then gently dip it into a small amount of sugar on a shallow plate. If the recipe does not call for citrus, so you don't have it handy, a small pastry brush dipped in syrup will work as well.

SPICY HERB GARDEN SALT

Makes 1½ cups

½ cup kosher salt

⅓ cup piment d'Espelette
or paprika

3 tablespoons ground
dried rosemary

3 tablespoons ground dried thyme

2 tablespoons coarse sea salt flakes,
such as Maldon brand

¾ teaspoon garlic powder

2¾ teaspoons onion powder

Equally good on eggs, avocado toast, chicken, and to season soups, this salt finishes the Michelada (page 224) and Bloody Mary (page 222).

Combine all the ingredients in a clean, dry glass jar, then seal with a lid. Store in a pantry or your home bar away from heat and light.

FENNEL POLLEN SALT

Makes 1½ cups

½ cup fennel buds (see directions)

1 cup coarse sea salt flakes, such as Maldon brand

If you read the Fennelcello introduction (page 109), you know why we were inspired to make this: abundance. Fennel pollen is an ingredient prized by chefs for its delicate yet complex notes of citrus, saffron, and anise. It's also something we tend to have a ton of each year, and it seemed a shame not to preserve it somehow.

A salt rim is perfect, because it not only adds a savory component to the Roman's Empire brunch cocktail (page 192) and an addictively salty-sweet thing to the Plenty Good shot (page 236), it is also a useful ingredient in your kitchen. Sprinkle it as a finishing salt on meat, fish, and pasta dishes. Belinda loves using it on top of creamy soups.

Snip a flower head off a fennel stalk. With a pair of sharp scissors, cut across the thin green stems that hold the yellow fennel buds and discard the thicker green stems below the buds. Gather about ½ cup of these buds. We keep the buds intact and don't mind some of the green stems, as these hold their own flavor and add an additional color and texture to the salt. Alternatively, you can also choose to shake the fennel pollen from the buds onto parchment. This will yield only the yellow pollen, and much less of it, but it will still be full of flavor. Add these to the coarse salt in a clean, dry glass jar, seal, and store.

148

FLORAL SALT OR SUGAR

Makes 1¼ cups

¼ cup dried edible floral petals

1 cup coarse raw or turbinado sugar

Choose sweet or salty based on the type of drinks you plan to make most often: the Margarita (page 190) and the Cock's Crow (page 228) love a salt rim, while sweet-tart drinks in the sour category, such as Fresh Lemonade by the Pitcher (page 168), Cordial Spritz (page 169), Cucumber Basil Gimlet (page 216), or Back Porch Lemonade (page 219) benefit from a sugar rim. This is another recipe that pulls equal weight for drinks and desserts; don't hesitate to use this liberally as a decorating salt or sugar.

Follow the instructions for Drying Flowers for Tea (page 122) to dry your flowers. Separate the petals from the centers, sepals, and any leaves and keep only the petals. Using several paper towels, wipe out a coffee grinder thoroughly, removing all coffee residue. Grind the dried flowers in the coffee grinder until fine, with some coarse petals left for texture. Then, transfer the ground flowers to a clean glass jar, add the sugar, and seal with a lid. Store in a pantry or your home bar away from heat and light.

HERB SUGAR

Makes 1½ cups

½ cup fresh herbs, or fir or spruce tips

1 cup coarse sugar

An unexpected sweet-herbal combination to rim sour and herbaceous cocktails, such as Fresh Lemonade by the Pitcher (page 168), Cordial Spritz (page 169), Spruce Drop (page 204), or Crown Jewel (page 205).

Wash and thoroughly dry the herbs or tips. Once completely dry, pour ½ cup of the sugar into a clean, dry glass jar add the herbs, then cover with the remaining ½ cup of sugar. Cover your jar and let the oils in the herb leaves infuse and flavor the sugar. Remove the herbs when the desired flavor is achieved. If left in the sugar too long, the herbs will wilt and turn brown, and the sweet fragrance of the oils will begin to taste off, like rot. Soft, leafy herbs, such as basil, will need only a few hours before you should remove and discard the leaves. Hardy herbs, such as rosemary, can infuse for days, up to a week before the herb is removed. To add additional texture, dehydrate or hang-dry herbs and add ¼ cup of coarsely chopped dried herbs to the herb-infused sugar. Store in a pantry or your home bar away from heat and light.

VANILLA SUGAR

Makes 3 cups

1 "spent" vanilla bean pod

3 cups coarse raw or turbinado sugar

This is equally versatile to rim sweet cocktails or use in baking; we top muffins and cookies with it, as well as the Apple Betty Martini (page 229) and Pumpkin Spice Espresso Martini (page 237). Because you'll use a real vanilla bean to make Whiskey-Soaked Cherries (page 95) and Pumpkin Spice Syrup (page 62), you may as well get multiple uses out of the bean. Despite your best efforts at thorough scraping of the tiny beans from the pod, plenty of flavor will remain clinging to it and will work wonders in this recipe.

TIP

You can use this vanilla bean pod one more time—it still has flavor to give. Place it in a small glass jar with 7 ounces of bourbon and let it infuse for 2 months to make your own vanilla extract.

On a cutting board, using a sharp paring knife, flatten out the vanilla bean pod and slice through the center to open it. Peel back from the center slit to open the pod, then drag the tip of your knife from the bottom to the top, scraping out the vanilla beans. Use these in another recipe. The pod alone, plus any of the tiny beans that remain clinging to it, will be enough to infuse the sugar strongly.

Pour half of the sugar into a clean, dry glass jar, add the vanilla bean pod, then cover with the remaining the sugar. Cover tightly, and the vanilla will infuse and flavor the sugar. Remove the vanilla pod after 1 to 2 weeks.

149

QUICK REFRIGERATOR PICKLES

We are aware that when the average person sees "pickles," they think of a jar of pickled cucumbers, probably with dill, the most common form of "pickle" in the USA. However, when we speak of pickling, it is in verb form and refers to all kinds of delicious pickled vegetables.

It's been said that Belinda will pickle anything that lets her, and experiments have ranged from the regular suspects to less common options, such as plums (so decadent for desserts and savory recipes, but the texture isn't great for an eating pickle), celery (delightful!), rhubarb (just all right), and watermelon rinds (not popular but not completely bad, either). Quick refrigerator pickles won't last for years the way water bath canned pickles can, but the tradeoff is their simplicity of preparation and their easy crispness, which can be lost when you heat pickles to can them in a water bath.

They're a great option for an easy cocktail garnish or a snack to have around, but because they last a month at most in the refrigerator, they are not a good choice if you're trying to preserve a large harvest or stock a kitchen pantry.

If you haven't already had this thought, let me put it in your mind: yes, you should drink the brine as pickleback after a shot of whiskey, or add some to a vodka martini served so cold it gives you shivers.

QUICK-PICKLED GARLIC SCAPES, ASPARAGUS, OR GREEN BEANS

Makes about 3 pints

1 pound vegetable of choice: asparagus, green beans, or scapes, trimmed

1 tablespoon black peppercorns

1 tablespoon coriander seeds

1 tablespoon mustard seeds

1 teaspoon red pepper flakes

2 cups water

3 cups rice vinegar or distilled white vinegar

3 tablespoons sea salt, plus more for blanching

2 tablespoons granulated cane sugar

6 garlic cloves, peeled and sliced

1 tablespoon lemon zest

Served alongside other cocktail hour snacks, the salty, lightly spicy pickles will help you finish your drink faster—as if that were an actual problem that people have. This one brine is quite versatile for a variety of crispy green vegetables. Use it all year to pickle through the seasons, from spring asparagus to summer beans.

Scapes are the curly green, aboveground growth of garlic. They should be cut after growing in late spring/early summer so that the energy of the garlic plant goes back underground into forming fat bulbs. Then, eat them, and you just may discover your new favorite vegetable. Scapes taste like milder garlic, but have a crisp crunch and shape similar to that of a green bean. They are available for a very short window of time every year at farmers' markets.

Prepare the vegetables by washing them and snipping off the ends.

Make the brine: Toast the peppercorns, coriander seeds, mustard seeds, and red pepper flakes in a small saucepot over low heat for 30 to 60 seconds, until the spices are fragrant. Make the brine: Add the water, vinegar, salt, and sugar and increase the heat to medium-high. Stir until the salt and sugar dissolve. Lower the heat to low and let the brine sit until your pickle jars are packed and ready for the brine to be added.

Meanwhile, blanch the veggies. Have ready a big salad bowl filled with ice water. In a separate pot, boil water with sea salt and then lightly dunk the vegetables into the boiling water for no more than 30 seconds. Remove the pot from the heat, drain the vegetables with a slotted spoon, then drop them into the ice bath. (This will quickly cool the vegetables so they maintain a crisp crunch.)

Remove the brine from the heat. Pack the blanched vegetables tightly into two or three pint-size mason jars or recycled, clean glass jars with tight-fitting lids. (Cut long asparagus in half if needed.) Evenly divide garlic and lemon zest and add them to the jars. Pour the brine over the top. It should cover the top of the veggies so they are submerged.

Cap with a lid and store in the refrigerator. The pickles will be full of flavor and ready to eat after 3 days, and best within a month.

NOTE: For milder pickles, omit the red pepper flakes. For spicier pickles, include ½ sliced jalapeño with seeds, divided between the jars.

PICKLED CARROTS

Makes about 3 pints

1 teaspoon coriander seeds

1 teaspoon black peppercorns

1 teaspoon red pepper flakes

1 cup rice vinegar or distilled white vinegar

1 cup water

2 tablespoons granulated cane sugar

1 tablespoon sea salt

1 pound carrots

2 garlic cloves, peeled and sliced

2 sprigs fresh thyme

Lemon peel from 1 lemon

Confession: We've never canned pickled carrots, but regrets? None. Fresh, they stay crunchier than canned pickled carrots ever could, and they are very easy to prep, so you can keep a jar in the fridge often. The carrots as prepared in this recipe are a little spicy, though you can omit the red pepper if you want a milder pickle; the lemon peel and herbs will give them a lot of flavor, regardless. The obvious choice is to serve these with the Bloody Bunny cocktails (page 201), but they are also delicious alongside the Garden Gibson (page 202) or in Bloody Mary Skewers (page 140).

Combine the coriander seeds, peppercorns, and red pepper flakes in a small saucepot and toast over low heat for 30 or 60 seconds, until fragrant. Make the brine: Add the vinegar, water, sugar, and salt and increase the heat to medium-high. Stir until the salt and sugar dissolve, then remove from the heat.

Peel and trim the carrots, then pack them tightly into two to three pint-size mason jars or recycled, clean glass jars with tight-fitting lids. Evenly divide garlic, thyme, and lemon peel and distribute them equally among the jars. Pour the brine over the top. It should cover the carrots so they are submerged. Cap with a lid and store in the refrigerator. The pickles will be full of flavor and ready to eat after 3 days, and best within a month.

153

PICKLED CUCAMELONS

Makes about 3 pints

1 pound cucamelons

1 tablespoon black peppercorns

2 cups water

3 cups cider vinegar

2 tablespoons salt

2 tablespoons granulated cane sugar

1 teaspoon lime zest

Let's get this out of the way: Cucamelons are adorable, like watermelons that have been put through a shrinking machine. They make the cutest garnish, either fresh or pickled. They don't stay crisp for long when they're fresh, so pickling them is a good way to get more adorableness on the side of your glass, longer. Cucamelons, aka Mexican sour gherkins, have a really unique flavor that is delicate like a cucumber but also a little lemony. Fresh, they pop in your mouth with a delightful little burst like a cherry tomato, and pickled they will keep this crunchy-juicy quality for an additional couple of weeks. Using a cider vinegar will bring out a little sweetness and keeping the brine simple will allow their flavor to come through.

Put a bowl of these on a cocktail table and they will quickly disappear, or spear three of them on a long bar pick and garnish savory cocktails.

Wash the cucamelons and leave them whole. Toast the peppercorns in a small saucepot over low heat for 30 to 60 seconds, until fragrant. Make the brine: Add the water, vinegar, salt, and sugar and increase the heat to medium-high, stirring until the salt and sugar dissolve. Add the toasted peppercorns and remove the brine from the heat.

Pack the cucamelons tightly into two or three pint-size mason jars or recycled, clean glass jars with tight-fitting lids. Evenly divide the zest and add it to the jars. Pour the brine over the top. It should cover the cucamelons. Cap with a lid and store in the refrigerator. The pickles will be ready to eat after 2 days, and best within 2 weeks.

155

QUICK-PICKLED GARLIC DILL CUCUMBERS

Makes about 3 pints

1 pound cucumbers

3 tablespoons salt

1 tablespoon black peppercorns

1 tablespoon coriander seeds

1 tablespoon mustard seeds

1 teaspoon red pepper flakes

2 cups water

3 cups rice vinegar or distilled white vinegar

2 tablespoons granulated cane sugar

6 garlic cloves, peeled and sliced

2 sprigs fresh dill

Quick pickling cucumbers speeds up the process so it's practical to make only a few jars at a time, unlike canning, which is a more time-consuming and precise process. Canning is more of a roll-up-your-sleeves, clean-the-kitchen, and make a batch of 6, 12, or possibly 148 jars of something at a time endeavor, depending on the kind of family you come from. With these, you can easily reduce or multiply the recipe, making as little as one jar at a time in 30 minutes or less.

For the crunchiest cucumbers, the effort of drawing moisture out with salt is worth it.

Prepare the cucumbers by slicing them into thin rounds and placing them in a colander. Sprinkle them with 1 tablespoon of the salt, cover them with a layer of ice, and toss cucumbers with your hands to mix with the salt and ice. Place the colander in the sink and let it sit for 30 minutes while you prepare the brine. This step pulls water from the cucumbers while keeping them chilled and will make your pickles crunchier.

Combine the peppercorns, coriander seeds, mustard seeds, and red pepper flakes in a small saucepot over low heat and toast for 30 to 60 seconds, until the spices are fragrant. Make the brine: Add the water, vinegar, and remaining salt and sugar and increase the heat to medium-high. Stir until the salt and sugar dissolve, then remove the brine from the heat.

Rinse the salt from the cucumbers by mixing them with your hands under running water. Keep rinsing until you taste a slice and it isn't salty. Pack the cucumbers tightly into two or three pint-sized mason jars or recycled, clean glass jars with tight fitting lids. Evenly divide the chopped garlic and dill and add them to the jars. Pour the brine over the top. It should cover the cucumbers so they are submerged. Cap with a lid and store in the refrigerator. The pickles will be full of flavor and ready to eat after 3 days, and best within a month.

PICKLED
CELERY

Makes about 3 pints

1 teaspoon black peppercorns

½ teaspoon celery seeds

2 cups rice vinegar or distilled white vinegar

1 cup water

1 tablespoon sea salt

3 tablespoons granulated cane sugar

1 pound celery

Our first celery shrub taught us how added tanginess from vinegar and a fresh celery juice could concentrate celery flavor. Yes, celery has a flavor, not just a texture, and we were knocked sideways with surprise by how good it could be! Pickles were the natural extension, another method to coax out the flavor that is muted by the fresh vegetable's high water content. Both the shrub and pickles magnify the celery flavor as if you are somehow crunching five celery sticks at once, something we all know would not be an exciting challenge for the average human mouth. The point here is that pickles erase the woes of celery, usually a fibrous, stringy crunch that exhausts the eater and has too much water to really let much flavor come through; this recipe turns celery on its head. It's pretty much a requirement that you use these pickles to garnish the Verde Maria (page 224) and Celery Shrub (page 74).

Combine the peppercorns and celery seeds in a small saucepot and toast over low heat for 30 to 60 seconds, until the spices are fragrant. Make the brine: Add the water, vinegar, sea salt, and sugar and increase the heat to medium-high. Stir until the salt and sugar dissolve. Add the toasted spices and remove the brine from the heat. Wash and trim the celery ribs, then cut them on the bias into ½-inch slices, holding your knife at a 45-degree angle to each rib so you get a slice with a lot of surface area. Pack the celery slices tightly into two or three pint-size mason jars or recycled, clean glass jars with tight-fitting lids. Pour the hot brine over the top. It should cover the celery slices so they are submerged. Cap with a lid and store in the refrigerator. The pickles will be full of flavor and ready to eat after 2 days, and best within 1 month.

157

PICKLED CHIVE
BLOSSOMS

Makes 1 half-pint jar,
about 8 ounces

1 cup fresh chive blossoms

6 ounces distilled white or red
wine vinegar

The vinegar and the blossoms
star in the Garden Gibson
(page 202), and the blossoms
can also be used to garnish
the Bloody Mary (page 222),
Michelada (page 224), or Verde
Maria (page 224).

Violet-purple chive blossoms will grow on the tops of your chives in summer, from May to August, and should be snipped or pinched off throughout the season to encourage more growth. Then, eat them! The whole chive plant is edible and the blossoms taste like delicate onions. Even if you have no intention of using these pickled chive blossoms in cocktails—and let us be clear that you should—do it for the vinegar.

Soaking the chive blossoms in vinegar dyes it the prettiest purple and lends the tangy vinegar a savory, umami flavor (*umami* means "essence of deliciousness" in Japanese). It's the type of ingredient you can pull out of your pantry to cook with and feel like a five-star chef, even though a toddler could prepare these.

In addition to being savory cocktail garnishes, the blossoms can also be used in salads; the vinegar in meat dishes to deglaze and make a pan sauce; and both work well in vegetable dishes (absolutely add these to deviled eggs and potato salad).

Wash the chive blossoms and then place them in a clean half-pint-size glass jar. Pour in the vinegar. Cap and store in the pantry and begin using after 5 days. The longer the chives sit in vinegar, the more flavor it develops and the more purple it will become. When the flavor is strong, strain out the chives. Flavored vinegars are fermented and so acidic that they are self-preserving and can be stored indefinitely, though flavor and appearance can change. The product will be freshest within 1 year, or until the expiration date of the vinegar you used in the recipe.

NON-ALCOHOLIC DRINKS

STRAWBERRIES AND CREAM SODA

Serves 1

3 strawberries

1½ ounces Strawberry Syrup
(page 50), Blackberry and Mint
Syrup (page 51), or preferred syrup

6 ounces seltzer

1 ounce half-and-half

0% ABV

---

*ELEVATE YOUR
MOCKTAIL*

Add a few drops of Distilled
Floral Water (page 127).

Garnish with a sprig of
basil or mint.

Serve with Fancy Ice (page 135).

A gaggle of children will run after you with excitement if you tell them you're making a batch of these; we know from experience. If you want some peace and quiet, this is not the drink to make—or keep it a secret if you do! The fresh local strawberries, which are available each June at farmers' market stands and U-Picks in the valley below our farm, are small, superjuicy, and bursting with sweetness. Their unparalleled taste is short lived, as they will become overripe and spoil in just a few days, so they demand you feast on them when you can. The berries don't travel well and they don't grow out of season, so you have to just stuff as many of them as you can into your drinks and meals in late June.

We actually love that about them. Not much is inconvenient and rare and therefore truly special in the modern food world, which often centers on fast and convenient food, but these strawberries are something to be savored. Indulge in the moment with these sodas.

Gently wash and dry the strawberries and remove the green stems. Muddle the strawberries at the bottom of a collins glass and add a scoop of crushed ice. Add the syrup, top with the seltzer, and stir gently. Drizzle in the half-and-half and stir once before serving.

163

SIMPLE SYRUP SODA

Serves 1

1½ ounces preferred syrup

6 ounces seltzer

0% ABV

A soda stream or a carbonating seltzer bottle makes seltzer at home accessible and easy, but the syrups that are sold commercially leave a lot to be desired in both taste and health. Ditch the dyes and corn syrup and make your own syrups, allowing for a world of flavors, and in addition, you can reduce the amount of syrup to control your sugar intake. Half an ounce of syrup will yield a lightly flavored seltzer, with an average of only 20 calories; ½ ounce of syrup with 1 ounce of fresh juice will have an even more robust flavor, and a full shot of syrup will make for a sweeter, traditional soda pop—still with fewer calories and more fiber, and far healthier overall than most commercial sodas.

Combine both ingredients in a collins glass full of crushed ice. Stir gently.

ELEVATE YOUR MOCKTAIL

Serve with Fancy Ice (page 135).

Reduce the syrup to half and replace with a fresh, tart-sweet juice, such as orange, grapefruit, or cranberry juice.

Add a few drops of Herb Tincture (page 86) or Pepper Tincture (page 87) for a final ABV of less than 0.5 percent.

164

SHRUB SODA

Serves 1

1 ounce preferred shrub or oxymel

6 ounces seltzer

0% ABV

It's the healthiest soda possible! Use a a shrub recipe from pages 68 to 80 to make this. A shrub soda is the colonial-era soda that assuages a sweet tooth while balancing the stomach with naturally fermented vinegar, aiding digestion. Not all palates will love these, but if you're like Belinda and love pickles and don't mind kombucha, you're going to fall fast for the sweet-sour combination of shrub sodas.

Combine the shrub and seltzer in a collins glass full of crushed ice. Stir gently. Garnish.

ELEVATE YOUR MOCKTAIL

The acidity of shrubs can be sharp; soften it with a Floral Sugar rim (page 148) on the glass or add a Candied Citrus Peel garnish (page 136).

Don't love bubbles? Reduce the seltzer by half and replace it with the same amount of a Botanical Water (page 119).

BITTERS & SODA

Serves 1

4 drops Barkeep's Citrus Bitters
(page 89) or Herb Tincture (page 86)

6 ounces seltzer

⅛ lime or lemon wedge

Garnish: Herb Bouquet (page 141)

0.1% ABV

Bitters and tinctures are like the salt and pepper of drinks—a little goes a long way to make plain carbonated water more exciting. With a little fresh citrus added, these just may be the refreshing drink that cures your canned, flavored seltzer addiction.

Sugar-free and known historically to aid digestion, a bitters and soda has long been the suggested tummyache cure from bartenders. Bitters are made and used in a manner similar to vanilla extract, and the amount of both present in a final recipe is so minimal that the final alcohol content is less than 1 percent.

Combine the bitters and seltzer in a collins glass full of crushed ice. Squeeze in the juice from the citrus wedge. Stir gently. Garnish.

NOTE: If you're avoiding all alcohol completely, substitute Distilled Floral Water (page 127) for the bitters or tincture.

ELEVATE YOUR MOCKTAIL

Add balanced sweetness: make it a collins-style mocktail with ½ ounce of Oleo Saccharum with Herbs (page 58), Citrus Cordial (page 59), or the syrup of your choice.

Don't love bubbles? Reduce the seltzer by half (some carbonation is necessary to keep the drink light) and replace it with the same amount of a Botanical Water (page 119).

Serve with Fancy Ice (page 135).

166

NONALCOHOLIC BUCK

Serves 1

1 ounce nonalcoholic spirit,
or club soda

2 to 3 drops Barkeep's Citrus Bitters
(page 89)

Optional: Up to ½ ounce preferred
syrup, such as Cranberry Rosemary
(page 65), Spruce (or Fir) Tip Syrup
(page 53), or Foraged Elderflower
Cordial (page 61)

1½ ounces No-Waste Spiced Lime
Shrub (page 75)

⅛ lime wedge

3 ounces club soda

Garnish: dried ginger slice on a
toothpick, or a sprig of fresh herb to
match the syrup of choice

0.1% ABV

---

*ELEVATE YOUR
MOCKTAIL*

Muddle in some fresh fruit or
herbs to add an additional layer
of freshness.

Add a few drops of Pepper
Tincture (page 87) or Herb
Tincture (page 86) for a final
ABV of 0.2%.

One of the simplest ways to make a nonalcoholic drink incredibly satisfying is to add spice, which mimics the spicy heat of liquor and has a really robust flavor. Ginger is a fantastic nonalcoholic drink ingredient for this reason, and the No-Waste Spiced Lime Shrub, aka Ginger Switchel (page 75) makes the tastiest nonalcoholic buck. We add a couple of drops of Barkeep's Citrus Bitters (page 89) to the nonalcoholic version for balance and complexity, but skip this step to preserve a 0% ABV for anyone avoiding all alcohol completely.

Fill a copper mule mug or old-fashioned glass with ice to overflowing. Pour in the nonalcoholic spirit of choice, bitters, syrup (if using), and shrub. Stir. Top with club soda. Squeeze the juice from the lime wedge into the cocktail. Stir again before garnishing.

167

FRESH LEMONADE BY THE PITCHER

Serves 4

8 ounces freshly squeezed lemon juice

8 ounces Blackberry and Mint Syrup (page 51) or preferred syrup

16 to 24 ounces water, to your preference, to dilute

4 cups ice

Garnishes: 1 lemon, sliced into thin rounds, plus 4 edible flowers

0% ABV

ELEVATE YOUR MOCKTAIL

Add a Floral Sugar rim (page 148) to your glass.

Garnish with Herb Bouquets (page 141).

Add ½ teaspoon of Distilled Floral Water (page 127) to your lemonade for a sophisticated nonalcoholic drink.

Add a few drops of Herb Tincture (page 86) for a final ABV of 0.1%.

Our dad taught us, "Always stop at a lemonade stand," with a seriousness akin to "always tell the truth." Maybe the lesson is to support the ventures of our littlest community members, or maybe it's to leave time in the journey for a spontaneous stop, or to make time in your day for sweet, simple things. You never know with our dad, but I suspect it's all of the above.

One day last summer, Belinda saw a stand and hooted at her husband to go around the block and pull up. After 10 years of marriage, he knew the drill, and when they came around, they were greeted by a toy plastic cash register, two towheaded little girls, and fresh lemonade. Imagine her delight when the little girl and her sister asked about their preferred flavor, then added our own product, a Simple Goodness Sisters Syrup, to her glass. Then, the intrepid young entrepreneur told Belinda about their big plans to buy a first-class plane ticket to California with their earnings so they could travel like queens. The story was touching and the drink was perfect. The lesson holds: always stop at a lemonade stand.

Combine the lemon juice, syrup, and water in a large pitcher and stir well. Serve chilled and over ice. Garnish with edible flowers and a lemon slice rested on the glass rim. Do not let the lemon slice stay submerged in the liquid for a long time before serving, or bitterness from the rind's pith will affect the beverage.

CORDIAL SPRITZ

Serves 1

1½ ounces Citrus Cordial (page 59), Lilac Cordial (page 60), or Foraged Elderflower Cordial (page 61)

¾ ounce freshly squeezed lemon juice

6 ounces seltzer (see Note about substituting tonic water)

Garnishes: 3 thin cucumber slices, 2 mint sprigs (trimmed to 1 inch long)

0% ABV

This hits all the right notes: tall, juicy, refreshing, and light. It will fulfill a gin and tonic craving. Amplify the juiciness of the sweet cordial by adding freshly squeezed citrus. You can use any of the cordial recipes found on pages 59 to 61.

Combine the cordial and lemon juice in a tall, stemmed wineglass filled with ice, then top with the seltzer and stir gently. Add the garnishes to the glass. Serve with a straw.

NOTE: We love elevating a cordial spritz with a stemmed glass and garnishes that you might traditionally see in a Spanish Gin & Tonic. Here, we've used thinly sliced cucumber and mint, but you could also choose thyme sprigs, edible flowers, dried juniper berries, or citrus peels or slices. Could you sub tonic in place of seltzer for added bitterness to meet a Gin & Tonic craving? Absolutely, but if you do, dial back the cordial to ½ ounce, because American tonic water has added sugar.

ELEVATE YOUR MOCKTAIL

Instead of adding the fresh juice, freeze it into ice cubes, which will slowly melt into the drink, flavoring it gradually.

Add Candied Citrus Peels (page 136).

Muddle in a fresh herb for layered flavor.

Add ½ teaspoon of Distilled Floral Water (page 127) or Herb Tincture (page 86). The Herb Tincture will raise the ABV to 0.1%.

Serve with Fancy Ice (page 135).

Garnish with an edible flower or an herb sprig.

169

ICED TEA

Serves 1

6 ounces brewed black tea, or other tea of your choosing, such as Sun Tea (page 126), chilled

1 ounce Lavender Honey Syrup (page 57) or preferred syrup

½ ounce freshly squeezed lemon juice

Garnishes: an edible flower, fresh mint leaf, and a lemon slice or curled lemon twist (see Notes)

0% ABV

We think Northerners have to grow into loving iced tea, whereas Southerners are born yearning for a sweating glass. As Scandinavian, Seattle area–born coffee drinkers, it's only recently that we've come to love a glass of iced tea as an afternoon pick-me-up after long hours on the farm. A flavored iced tea is also a wonderful way to curb a soda habit, with less sugar. Tea makes the perfect, slightly bitter tannic base for layering sweet garden syrups over, and you won't need a lot to get a great flavor. If you get into the habit of making a pint or two a week so it's readily at hand, we think you'll be surprised by how often you'll reach for it.

Combine all the ingredients, except the garnishes, in a cocktail shaker and shake over ice until the outside of the shaker is cold, about 15 seconds. Strain into a glass filled with fresh ice. Garnish with an edible flower, mint leaf, and lemon slice or twist.

NOTES: Prepare the tea to your preferred strength and allow it to cool at room temperature before chilling it; this will prevent the tea from clouding (although cloudy tea is still perfectly safe to drink, if you don't have the time to spare).

To make the lemon twist, use a sharp paring knife to remove a 2-inch segment of lemon peel, avoiding the white pith. Squeeze the lemon peel over the top of the glass with a pinch to express the oils, and then drop it in.

170

TRY THESE COMBINATIONS

CLASSIC
Prepared black tea + Citrus Cordial (page 59)

FLORAL
Prepared chamomile and calendula tea + Lavender Honey Syrup (page 57) or Lilac Cordial (page 60)

SWEET JULEP TEA
Prepared black tea + Blackberry and Mint Syrup (page 51)

ELEVATE YOUR MOCKTAIL

Make it an Arnold Palmer:
4 ounces cooled brewed tea, 1 ounce preferred syrup, 2 ounces water, and ¾ ounce freshly squeezed lemon juice.

Serve with Fancy Ice (page 135).

Garnish with a Citrus Wheel (page 138) or Herb Bouquet (page 141).

AT HIGH NOON

Serves 1

2 ounces Botanical Water of choice
(page 119)

2 ounces coconut water

3 ounces freshly squeezed Green
Juice (page 116), or grapefruit or
orange juice

Garnish: lime wedge

———————

0% ABV

There's no alcohol here, just the kind of refreshing drink you need to get through a hot summer's day. It can be drunk casually by the glass from a pitcher kept in the fridge or you can elevate it and serve it in a stemmed glass with a straw at an outdoor dinner party. This is a zero-proof drink with a loose format. Mix it up differently according to your mood and what's in your fridge. Just combine different Botanical Waters (page 119) and various freshly squeezed juices with a little coconut water for a richer mouthfeel and added electrolytes. This makes a thirst-quenching, nonbubbly mocktail that can also be used as a low-calorie mixer for cocktails.

Combine all the ingredients, except the garnish, in a collins glass full of crushed ice. Stir gently. Garnish with the lime wedge.

ELEVATE YOUR MOCKTAIL

Serve in a stemmed glass with ice and a straw. Pour in the ingredients in order for a layered effect: the juice first, followed by slowly pouring the coconut water over the back of a barspoon, then repeat with a slow pour of the Botanical Water.

Add 2 or 3 drops of Pepper Hot Sauce (page 81) as a spicy little wake-up.

Add a sprig of mint or an edible flower as a garnish.

Serve with Fancy Ice (page 135).

171

CREAMY TEA
COBBLER

Serves 1

¼ cup fresh berries or other fruit

1 ounce Blackberry and Mint Syrup
(page 51) or your preferred syrup

5 ounces Sun Tea (page 126) or
prepared black tea, cooled

½ ounce heavy whipping cream or
coconut cream

Garnish: fresh mint, fruit speared
on a toothpick

0% ABV

ELEVATE YOUR
MOCKTAIL

Add a couple of drops of Distilled
Floral Water (page 127).

Freeze fresh or dried fruit into
your ice cubes (page 135).

Garnish with a toothpick of
Mojito Berries (page 144).

A riff on the traditionally low-alcohol-content sherry cobbler cocktails (which pioneered the use of straws and crushed ice in cocktails!) and British milky teas, this cobbler is alcohol-free but lacking nothing. Whip one up for a perfect afternoon or after-dinner pick-me-up.

Use this recipe as a formula, liberally substituting different syrup flavors for each season. Switch out the fruit, syrups, and tea for a wide variety of possibilities. Mint or lemongrass syrup with green tea, muddled blueberries, and coconut milk will transport you, and Lavender Honey Syrup (page 57) with Earl Grey tea and cream is classic.

Place the fresh fruit in a collins glass or stemless wineglass and muddle. Fill to the top with crushed ice. Add the syrup, then slowly pour in the tea. Pour in the heavy whipping cream, stirring once in the middle of the pour for dramatic effect. (Use only whipping cream, as half-and-half and other lower-fat dairy milks will likely curdle due to the acidity of the fruit.) Add the garnishes.

NOTE: Low pH from acidic syrups and teas can cause the proteins in milk to coagulate and curdle. While unsightly, it is perfectly safe to drink. To avoid clumping, use full-fat dairy and stir in the cream slowly. It also helps to choose less-acidic syrups and teas, avoiding in particular the Citrus Cordial, Oleo Saccharum, and Lime Basil Syrup in this recipe.

173

DIRTY SODA AND THE CLASSIC EGG CREAM

Serves 1

8 ounces preferred soda pop, such as Coca-Cola, or substitute plain seltzer for an egg cream

1 ounce preferred syrup

1 small lime wedge (optional)

1 ounce heavy cream, coconut cream, or nondairy creamer

0% ABV

Soda fountains have been serving a combo of flavored syrup and carbonated water since the late 1800s in America. Today, sodas are mass produced in cans or bottles, and no one gives them a second thought. Back then, though, sodas were mixed on demand—using syrup and carbonated water—and served over ice. This was a treat in and of itself before refrigeration and freezers had reached homes, when ice was a rarity.

In 1874, the classic syrup-plus-seltzer combo got an upgrade. Syrup, seltzer, and sweet cream combined for the first time, creating the ice cream soda. This evolved into another drink, the egg cream, made with milk or half-and-half as a lower-cost alternative to the ice cream soda.

You can combine seltzer with any syrup, alternative milk, milk, or cream, and any fruit or spice garnishes, and end up with hundreds of egg cream possibilities. If you begin with cola soda products and then add syrup and cream, you've got the modern social media trend of "dirty soda."

If you start with seltzer and do not add acidity from citrus juices, you can use whole milk, alternative milks, or half-and-half.

Fill a pint-size glass to the top with crushed or pebbled ice. Add the soda pop or seltzer. Add the syrup and stir gently. Squeeze in the lime juice, if desired. Stir. Add the cream on top and let it run down into the soda. Crushed ice is important here!

NOTE: Use only heavy cream, coconut cream, or nondairy creamer if you're using an acidic soda pop, such as cola, or adding the freshly squeezed lime juice. Full-fat dairy will help prevent curdling from the soda pop's acidity.

FLAVOR COMBINATIONS TO TRY

STRAWBERRY DREAM
Strawberry Syrup (page 50) + Coca-Cola or Dr Pepper + coconut cream

PUMPKIN PIE EGG CREAM
Pumpkin Spice Syrup (page 62) + seltzer + whole milk or half-and-half

WEST COAST EGG CREAM
Lavender Honey Syrup (page 57) + seltzer + oat milk

LOAF CAKE EGG CREAM
Citrus Cordial (page 59) + seltzer + almond milk

ITALIAN SUMMER DIRTY SODA
Lime Basil Syrup (page 54) + Coca-Cola + heavy cream

ELEVATE YOUR MOCKTAIL

Create a layered look by starting with the ice, then pouring in the syrup first, then slowly adding the club soda, and finally pouring the half-and-half slowly over the back of a barspoon on top.

Top with a complementary infused whipped cream: Add a shot of syrup to 12 ounces of heavy whipping cream, then charge with an iSi whip canister, or use a bowl and handheld mixer to whip into stiff peaks.

Freeze dried flowers or fruit into Fancy Ice (page 135).

HOT SPICED CIDER

Serves 8

1 cinnamon stick, broken
into pieces

¼ star anise pod

2 cloves

1 allspice berry, cracked

¼ teaspoon dehydrated orange peel

64 ounces Fresh-Pressed Apple
Cider (page 114)

Optional: 1 ounce vodka, whiskey,
or rum; and 1 ounce Orchardist
Liqueur (page 107) per serving

Garnish: 1 whole nutmeg, grated, to
top, dried Citrus Wheels (page 138)
or Candied Citrus Peels (page 136)

0% ABV

ELEVATE YOUR MOCKTAIL

Serve in glass mugs with handles
and float a Candied Citrus Peel
(page 136) or dried Citrus Wheel
(page 138) on top.

Add a splash of orange juice
to each glass, or 12 drops
of Barkeep's Citrus Bitters
(page 89) to balance the sweet
cider (with bitters, the final ABV
will be 0.1%).

The addition of aromatic baking spices and a cozy temperature change freshly pressed apple cider into a drink your guests will come back for more. A simmering pot full of this hot spiced cider will make your home smell incredible as it heats, and the taste couldn't be more comforting, or further apart from that powdered apple sugar packet that always settles to the bottom of your mug in a grainy finish. We love making this for fall harvest parties and snow days, or filling a thermos before trick-or-treating or snowshoeing.

Remember: You can water bath can cider for shelf stability and year-round enjoyment, or freeze it well for up to 3 months in jugs if you leave 20 percent of the volume empty to allow for expansion when the cider freezes. So, feel free to make larger batches! If you don't want to bother with the dehydrated orange peel, add 2 tablespoons of orange juice.

Serve it warm, either by reheating already prepared spiced cider in individual servings, or for a party, keep a big batch in a stockpot over low heat or in a slow cooker on LOW. If serving with alcohol, add it just before serving. Do not let it simmer or boil, or you could lower the potency. Place mugs or teacups near the stovetop or slow cooker and serve with a ladle.

175

Combine the cinnamon stick, star anise, cloves, and allspice berry in a clean, dry pan and toast over low heat until fragrant, 30 to 60 seconds. Heat the cider in a separate pot over medium-low heat or in a microwave until hot but not boiling. Add the toasted spices and orange peel, stir, and let infuse for 5 minutes. Remove from the heat.

Remove the spices with a slotted spoon or by straining the hot cider, then serve warm. If adding alcohol, pour 8 ounces of cider into a mug, then add in 1 ounce of vodka, whiskey, or dark rum along with 1 ounce of Orchardist Liqueur, for a finished ABV of 6%. Sprinkle the grated nutmeg on top of each serving and add a dried citrus wheel or candied peel for a nice color-contrasting garnish that won't impart any competing flavors.

ALTERNATIVE BATCHED COCKTAIL

10 servings/80 ounces: Heat 64 ounces of cider in a slow cooker set to LOW, or in a pot over medium-low heat, until heated but not simmering. Add just before serving: 10 ounces of Orchardist Liqueur (page 107) and 10 ounces of vodka, and stir. Add dried Citrus Wheels (page 138) to the top for a nice color-contrasting garnish that won't impart any competing flavors. Place mugs or teacups near the stovetop or slow cooker and serve with a ladle.

ICED COFFEE

Serves 1

1 ounce Pumpkin Spice Syrup
(page 62), Lavender Honey Syrup
(page 57), or preferred syrup

1 ounce half-and-half

5 ounces cold-brew coffee

Garnish: infused whipped cream
(recipe follows; optional)

0% ABV

*ELEVATE YOUR
MOCKTAIL*

Create a layered look by adding
ice first, then pouring in the cold
brew and syrup; stir. Pour the
half-and-half on top and let it run
down into the ice.

Top with freshly grated nutmeg,
cinnamon, or a sprinkle of
crushed, dried edible flower
petals, depending on your syrup
flavor of choice.

Get even fancier with your
grated spice or edible flower
petals by using a sheet of paper
to block two-thirds of the
glass and sprinkle only on the
open side, leaving a crisp line
between the garnish and the
whipped cream.

Where we live an hour's drive from Seattle, there is a coffee shop on every corner, and the drink menus are as inventive as the winter daylight hours are short. We reach for this iced coffee to wake up, and while Belinda chooses Lavender Honey Syrup (page 57), Venise loves it with Pumpkin Spice Syrup (page 62). It's our everyday drinker, made extra cozy because the flavors are preserved from last season's garden.

Mix up the syrups and milks to fit your mood. You can even mess around with pairing the coffee's tasting notes with the rest of the drink, such as making your coffee with a bright, South American coffee with berry and chocolate notes, and pairing it with a raspberry or currant syrup. Classic syrups, such as cinnamon or vanilla, are also great.

Infusing your whipped cream with a flavor before whipping it can take your drink one very special step further.

If you don't care for coffee, you can sub in a strongly brewed iced black tea here and get a delicious morning caffeine hit your own way.

Combine all the ingredients, except the garnish, in a glass of ice and stir. Top with infused whipped cream, if desired.

INFUSED WHIPPED CREAM

12 servings: In an iSi whip canister, combine 1½ ounces syrup that will complement your iced coffee with 12 ounces heavy whipping cream. Shake before you charge with a gas cartridge. Alternatively, use a stand mixer with a small bowl or a handheld mixer with a small bowl. Chilling the bowl in advance in the fridge for 20 minutes will help the cream whip faster. Whip the cream and syrup on the highest setting until peaks form (this is when the beaters leave ridges and peaks in the cream as they beat, instead of a smooth or lumpy surface). Store in the refrigerator in a sealed container until ready to use. Use within 5 days.

COCKTAILS

HARD SELTZER OR RANCH WATER

Serves 1

1 (8-ounce) can or glass bottle of seltzer

1 ounce silver tequila or potato vodka, or substitute a nonalcoholic spirit of choice for a mocktail

¼ to ½ ounce of any flavor of preferred syrup

Garnish: wedge of lime

5% ABV

A few summers back, one 98°F day, we took a trip down a narrow gravel road, butts bouncing and dust flying, over ruts and one evil stick that would lodge in the truck's wheel well and later cause a lot of grief, and ended at a riverbank in Montana. With our husbands and some cousins, we arrived at the bank, put our feet in the icy river, and poured a round of Ranch Waters, and to this day, I am not sure there has ever been a better cocktail consumed.

These no-fuss cocktails are incredibly convenient and fast to make, so we love them for a crowd and on location. As such, this minimalist drink is probably the recipe we make the most often in summer. It goes down easy after a long, hot day working on the farm and equally as well on a riverbank.

Making these at home versus buying the convenience cans will not only save money, but you can also improve the ingredients used, such as better-quality tequila for a tastier drink. These can be adapted to feature any of your garden-to-glass drink syrup flavors. Take them a step further by adding a Floral Salt or Sugar (page 148) rim, or by using one of your infused spirits.

Whether planning to mix multiple cocktails at home or on location, prechill your spirit, seltzer, two limes cut into wedges and stored in a sealed bag, and syrup in the fridge or in a cooler.

Open your seltzer and drink the first few ounces to make room—hydrating is important! Add the vodka and syrup and stir. If on location without any tools, measure with your heart. Serve the drink with a lime wedge stuffed into the can opening or bottle neck—squeeze it in before drinking.

SPARKLING ROSÉ WINE SPRITZER

Serves 1

4 ounces sparkling rosé wine, chilled

½ ounce Lilac Cordial (page 60)
or Foraged Elderflower Cordial
(page 61)

1 ounce club soda

Garnish: edible flower, lemon twist
(see Notes)

9% ABV

Light, bubbly, and easy to pour and serve to a group, a wine spritzer may be our most frequent flier of a spring or summer hosting cocktail. The lightness of a rosé wine allows the cordial's floral flavors to shine. A wine spritzer is lazy elegance at its peak, especially when you top the cocktail with an edible flower. They're especially easy to pack for a picnic and well suited for the times when you want to drink more than one but keep your total alcohol consumption in check.

Pour the chilled wine into a stemmed glass. Add the cordial and stir once. Top with a splash of club soda. Gently add a scoop of ice and garnish with an edible flower floating in the glass. Squeeze the lemon twist over the top of the cocktail.

NOTES: Make it nonalcoholic by substituting an alcohol-removed sparkling wine, such as Jøyus wine, or replace the wine with club soda and a few drops of Distilled Floral Water (page 127). A few drops of Barkeep's Citrus Bitters (page 89) or Herb Tincture (page 86) will result in a nearly alcohol-free drink as well.

To make a lemon twist, use a sharp paring knife or a Y-peeler to peel a 3-inch length of lemon rind, avoiding the white pith as much as possible. Squeeze the lemon peel over the top of the glass with a pinch to express the oils, and then drop it in.

182

BUCK

Serves 1

2 ounces vodka, rum, tequila, gin,
or bourbon

⅛ lime wedge

1 ounce No-Waste Spiced Lime
Shrub (page 75)

3 ounces club soda

Garnish: dried ginger slice on a
toothpick, or a sprig of fresh herb to
match the syrup of choice

12% ABV

In addition to being a male deer, a "buck" is a drink category whereby you combine a spirit with ginger ale or ginger beer plus a citrus drink. You can use any liquor, and we encourage you to try a few variations. These types of drinks are now commonly called "mules" in the USA, instead of "bucks," due to the popularity of the Moscow Mule, which is simply one type of buck cocktail made from vodka. The Moscow Mule was invented as a co-advertising tactic between a ginger beer and vodka brand. The No-Waste Spiced Lime Shrub (page 75) makes a homemade replacement for ginger beer when you add club soda, but if you want to make a buck and don't have that mixer made, you can sub in 4 ounces of ginger beer. To make it a mocktail, simply omit the spirit—it's delicious!

The copper mule mug is not necessary, though the copper will insulate the ice and keep the drink very cold, which is essential. If you don't have one, just be sure you fill the cup all the way to the top with ice.

Fill a copper mule mug or old-fashioned glass with ice to overflow the mug. Pour in your spirit of choice and shrub. Stir. Squeeze the juice from the lime wedge into the cocktail. Stir again before garnishing with ginger or a sprig of fresh herb.

183

RED SKIES
AT NIGHT

Makes 1

1 ounce No-Waste Spiced Lime
Shrub (page 75)

2 ounces dark aged rum, such as
Havana Club or Flor de Caña brand

3 ounces club soda

Garnish: 1 lime wedge

ABV 12%

---

*OTHER COMBINATIONS
TO TRY*

Blackberry and Mint
Syrup (page 51) + bourbon

Lime Basil Syrup (page 54)
+ light rum

Pumpkin Spice Syrup (page 62) +
spiced rum

Cranberry Rosemary Syrup
(page 65) + vodka

184

Sometimes, a drink defines a moment, a mood, or an event just perfectly, and that is the case with this drink. Red Skies at Night is our version of the famous Dark and Stormy, using the No-Waste Spiced Lime Shrub, aka Ginger Switchel (page 75). It's built for beachside or boat sipping.

The intensity of the shrub meets the depths of a spiced rum for a drink that is truly, as the saying goes, "a sailor's delight." Historically, rum or gin rations on British ships were made into a punch with fresh citrus juices for the vitamin C that helped ward off scurvy after months at sea without fresh produce, then flavored with exotic spice route spices such as clove and cinnamon.

Combine the shrub and spirit in a cocktail shaker with a scoop of ice. Cap and shake for 20 seconds. Strain the cocktail into a copper mule mug or old-fashioned glass filled to the top with fresh crushed ice. Top with club soda and stir once. Rest a lime wedge on the rim of the mug and serve with a straw.

LILAC AND LEAD FRENCH 75

Serves 1

1½ ounces Compound Gin (page 90) or any other botanical gin

½ ounce Lilac Cordial (page 60)

2 to 3 drops Distilled Floral Water (page 127) made with lilac (optional)

1 ounce freshly squeezed lemon juice

2 ounces Champagne

Garnish: lemon twist (see Note)

14% ABV

Make this with the Lilac Cordial (page 60), and you've got the Lilac and Lead. Its name is a play on the French 75's name origins from World War I, in honor of the then new technology of French artillery rifles that packed a punch, as does this drink. Lilac is a light flavor, so a few drops of distilled lilac water will help the lilac cordial come through the stronger profile of gin.

Think of the recipe as merely a jumping-off point: a French 75 can go in many directions by swapping out a new cordial or syrup, from huckleberry to melon, to grapefruit and peppercorn syrup, all with great success.

Combine the gin, cordial, lilac water, and lemon juice with 1 cup of ice in a cocktail shaker and shake. Strain into an old-fashioned glass filled with ice. Top with Champagne. Alternatively, you can strain this cocktail into a coupe or Champagne flute and serve it without ice for a faster-drinking and more elegant presentation. Leaving the ice in is less attractive, but many like it to dilute this alcohol-forward cocktail as you drink. Both versions have their benefits!

NOTE: To make the lemon twist, use a sharp paring knife to remove a 2-inch segment of lemon peel, avoiding the white pith. Squeeze the lemon peel over the top of the glass with a pinch to express the oils, and then drop it in.

MAKING HAY
SHANDY

Serves 1

12 ounces chilled light beer, such as
a pale ale or pilsner

1 ounce freshly squeezed lemon juice

1 ounce Citrus Cordial
(page 59), Oleo Saccharum with
Herbs (page 58), or Spruce Tip
Syrup (page 53)

ABV ~6%

This cocktail is an annual summer tradition on the farm. To feed the
goats and cows all winter, Venise's husband, Ross, spends many hours
making hay. Making hay requires hot, dry weather, which means that
when everyone else is enjoying the first hot days of summer at the lake,
Ross is driving circles in the hayfields. Once the hay is put into bales,
Venise and the kids all pitch in and load them onto a trailer and bring
them home. It is a dusty, sweaty, itchy job. Which is why, after the last
bale is unloaded into the barn, we celebrate with a tall glass of cold beer
cocktail. There is truly nothing as rewarding as a beer well earned and a
full barn of hay!

A shandy is made with beer mixed with citrus, lemonade, or lemon-
lime flavored sodas. The proportions differ and can be up to half beer,
half mix. We keep more beer in the mix here for a flavored beer that isn't
too sweet and is entirely refreshing and easy to drink on warm days.
You can play with the proportions, the syrup flavors, and the type of
citrus you use—lemon, lime, and grapefruit are all good choices, and
you should try swapping them to complement the beer you're using.
For instance, sweeter grapefruit juice is a good balance for a bitter IPA,
wheat beers and Hefeweizen are a natural choice for orange juice, whereas
lemon plays well with a domestic lager for easy sipping. Feel empowered
to experiment!

187

Pour the beer into a prechilled glass, leaving 2 inches of room at the top for
your mix-in of choice. Add the lemon juice to a chilled pint-size glass of beer.
Add the syrup and stir lightly.

MAKE IT NONALCOHOLIC: Use a nonalcoholic beer for an equally enjoyable
beverage full of body.

OLD-FASHIONED

Serves 1

3 drops/dashes Barkeeper's Citrus Bitters (page 89)

¼ ounce Oleo Saccharum with Herbs (page 58), Lavender Honey Syrup (page 57), Pumpkin Spice Syrup (page 62), or preferred simple syrup

One 2-inch square or round ice cube

2 ounces good bourbon or rye whiskey, to your preference

Orange peel

Club soda (optional)

Garnish: Whiskey-Soaked Cherries (page 95)

34% ABV

188

Before you get mad at us, let us be upfront: This recipe makes the common substitution of using a small amount of simple syrup in place of the sugar cube. It may seem sacrilegious to change up the classic old-fashioned formula, but bartenders do it all the time and you should, too! Other than using syrup to replace the sugar cube, which blends the cocktail better for no grainy bits at the bottom of the glass, this recipe is pretty traditional. It follows what we like to call the Old Bar style versus the *Mad Men* style of adding muddled cherry and an orange slice.

The original old-fashioned looked more like this recipe: no dilution other than ice for a strong sip. Then, in the 1950s, the garnish cherry began to be muddled with an orange slice instead of a citrus twist, and club soda was added. Midwesterners often use brandy instead of whiskey in theirs, and all of this is fine. We encourage you to make your old-fashioned reflect your own homeland.

We love to mix up our old-fashioneds throughout the seasons to reflect where we live, what we have growing, and the flavors we love. Using Oleo Saccharum with Herbs (page 58) as your syrup will give an orange flavor that may be more familiar.

Combine the bitters and syrup in a rocks glass and stir. Add the ice cube and pour in the bourbon. Stir gently 10 times. Rub the orange peel around the rim of the glass, then twist it with both hands to express the oils over the top of the cocktail and drop it into the glass. A small splash of club soda is optional, but will make the drink more enjoyable for some. Skewer a bourbon-soaked cherry with a toothpick and add it to the cocktail, swirling it once to incorporate the soda (if using).

MARGARITA

Serves 1

1½ ounces blanco tequila or Jalepeño Tequila (page 96)

½ ounce Oleo Saccharum with Herbs (page 58), Strawberry Syrup (page 50), Cranberry Rosemary Syrup (page 65), Pumpkin Spice Syrup (page 62), or other preferred syrup

½ ounce orange liqueur, such as Cointreau

1 ounce freshly squeezed lime juice

Garnish: Floral Salt (page 148), orange slice, and nasturtium or other edible flowers

18% ABV

MAKE IT A PUMPKIN SPICE MARGARITA

Omit the salt rim, use Pumpkin Spice Syrup (page 62) and garnish with freshly grated nutmeg.

You know who always has friends? Someone who has a pitcher of margaritas. So, make these by the pitcher. It's a classic for a reason. The only change we've made to the traditional recipe is to split the sweetness. Half comes from the simple syrup, so that you can add fun seasonal syrups to the recipe, instead of it all coming from an orange liqueur such as Cointreau. (You can use any orange liqueur, but we think that Cointreau is the best). Use 100 percent agave tequila and look for bottles that state the agave plants used to make the tequila were harvested at 5 or more years old. You can't make a silk purse out of a sow's ear, and the younger agave plants have less developed sugars and make for lower-quality tequila.

Love a spicy margarita? Add a few coins of fresh jalapeño peppers and muddle them in before shaking this drink, or add a few drops of Pepper Tincture (page 87).

Place 1 cup of ice in a cocktail shaker and add the tequila, oleo saccharum, orange liqueur, and lime juice. Shake the drink until the outside of the shaker is very cold, about 25 seconds. Rim a margarita or coupe glass with floral salt by placing the salt in a shallow dish, rubbing a small amount of spirit or citrus along the half of the rim of the glass, then gently rolling it in the salt. Fill the rimmed glass with ice. Strain the drink into the glass. Garnish with an orange slice and nasturtiums.

MAKE IT SPICY: Reduce the tequila to ¾ ounce and add ¾ ounce of Jalapeño Tequila (page 96). Garnish with a pepper so people know what to expect.

PITCHER MARGARITA

Makes 8 cocktails

12 ounces silver tequila

4 ounces syrup of choice

4 ounces orange liqueur, such as Cointreau

8 ounces freshly squeezed lime juice

2 ounces water

Garnish: Floral Salt (page 148), orange slices, and nasturtium or other edible flowers

Rim margarita or coupe glasses with floral salt by placing the salt in a shallow dish, rubbing a small amount of spirit or citrus along half of the rim of each glass, and gently rolling them in the salt. Combine the tequila, syrup, orange liqueur, lime juice, and water in a large pitcher and stir 10 times. Chill until ready to serve. Before serving, add enough ice to each glass to fill all the way up to the top. Pour 4 ounces of cocktail into each glass. Garnish the glasses with an orange slice and nasturtiums.

MAKE IT SPICY: Reduce the tequila to 6 ounces and add 6 ounces of Jalapeño Tequila (page 96). Garnish with a pepper so people know what they're getting.

BEE'S KNEES

Serves 1

2 ounces Buzz Button Gin (page 92)

¾ ounce Lavender Honey Syrup
(page 57)

¾ ounce freshly squeezed
lemon juice

Garnish: Herb Bouquet (page 141)

20% ABV

This Prohibition-era drink is especially buzz-worthy when made with Buzz Button Gin (page 92). The toothache plant–infused gin creates a tingling sensation that lasts just about 10 minutes and will build up stronger as you drink the cocktail. Las Vegas has introduced many drinkers to this sensation with a cocktail at its Cosmpolitan hotel, but you can grow your own at home.

Chill your coupe glass in the fridge, or quickly chill the glass by placing 1 cup of ice in the glass while you mix the drink. In a cocktail shaker, combine all the liquid ingredients plus another cup of the ice and shake until the outside of the shaker is very cold, about 20 seconds. If you added ice to the coupe to chill it, discard it now. Strain the cocktail into the chilled coupe. Garnish with an herb bouquet floating in the glass.

ROMAN'S EMPIRE

Serves 1

4 ounces freshly squeezed grapefruit
juice (from about 1 large grapefruit)

¾ ounce vodka

¾ ounce Fennelcello (page 109)

2 sprigs mint

1 tablespoon Fennel Pollen Salt
(page 148)

7% ABV

Belinda is forever trying to use fennel in ways that don't result in drinks that are too in-your-face with licorice, and this one achieves that: a fennel cocktail for beginners, if you will. Belinda's cocktail inspiration comes from everywhere, but especially food. No delightful meal, cookbook recipe, or restaurant menu is free from being run by the "Is there a cocktail somewhere in here?" section of her brain. Based on a salad by Alison Roman in her book *Dining In*, the combination of fennel, mint, and grapefruit seemed like the start of a brunch cocktail. Low in alcohol content, it's a feel-good start to a weekend morning. Freshly squeezed grapefruit juice, not bottled, makes all the difference. Juice those grapefruits and candy the rinds (page 136)!

Pour the grapefruit juice into a cocktail shaker. Add the vodka and Fennelcello, plus one of the mint sprigs (clap the mint between your hands before you drop it in). Cap and shake for 20 seconds. Place the fennel pollen salt in a shallow dish. Rim an old-fashioned glass by running the juiced side of the grapefruit along half of the rim of the glass, then gently dipping it into the salt. Add ice to fill the glass. Strain and pour the drink into the prepared glass and garnish with the other mint sprig.

WHITE SANGRIA

Serves 1

2 sprigs thyme (see Note)

½ ounce Citrus Cordial (page 59)

1 ounce Stone Fruit Tea (page 126)

1 ounce freshly squeezed
orange juice

½ ounce Elderflower Liqueur
(page 106)

3 ounces Viognier

Garnish: 1 sprig thyme

6% ABV

You know you've succeeded as a host when you get a text afterward asking for a recipe, and this sangria has that effect. Viognier is a full-bodied white wine that perfectly complements stone fruits in Stone Fruit Tea (page 126) and is bold enough to be mixed into this sangria without getting lost. If you can't find Viognier, use a not-too-buttery chardonnay. You can make this recipe with the stone fruit of your choice. Plums, nectarines, or peaches all work well.

Muddle the 2 sprigs of thyme into the cordial at the bottom of a wineglass. Add the stone fruit tea, juice, liqueur, and wine. Stir at least 10 times. Add ice until the glass is half full.

NOTE: There is no need to muddle in the thyme if you already added mint or thyme to your Stone Fruit Tea recipe. It will become overpowering, so skip that step.

PITCHER SANGRIA

Serves 8

½ cup fresh thyme

4 ounces Citrus Cordial (page 59)

8 ounces Stone Fruit Tea (page 126), chilled

8 ounces freshly squeezed orange juice, or strongly muddle 2 oranges

4 ounces Elderflower Liqueur (page 106)

One 25-ounce bottle Viognier, chilled

Ice

Garnish: 1 sprig thyme, Citrus Wheels (page 138)

Muddle the fresh thyme into cordial at the bottom of a pitcher. Add the stone fruit tea, juice, liqueur, and wine. Stir at least 10 times. Add ice until pitcher is half full. Garnish with a sprig of thyme and citrus wheels.

CLARIFIED MILK PUNCH

Serves 3

4½ ounces Compound Gin
(page 90) or other botanical gin

8 ounces (1 cup) brewed black tea

2 ounces Lavender Honey Syrup
(page 57)

2 ounces freshly squeezed
lemon juice

4 ounces (1 cup) milk

Fancy Ice (page 135)

Garnish: none, if using fancy
ice that contains edible flowers.
Otherwise a sprig of lavender in the
glass is a nice touch.

10% ABV

The art and science of preserving foods is ever fascinating to us. This cocktail is like a magic trick of nature our forefathers discovered. Plus, it tastes really good! Milk is an ancient way of preserving food that plays infrequently in modern day. In this punch, milk is made to curdle from the tannins in tea and acidity of the lemon juice, so that the milk proteins bind to the most bitter and astringent agents in alcohol before they're strained off. The result is the smoothest version of the spirit you can get, as well as a finished cocktail with a rich mouthfeel, which can be stored at room temperature for a year! Simple in presentation, this clear yellow cocktail with perfect clarity will surprise you with its complexity. Use the clarity of the cocktail to show off Fancy Ice (page 135) made with colorfast flowers (see page 35).

Combine the gin, tea, syrup, and lemon juice in a quart-size mason jar. Pour the milk into another mason jar. Add the gin mixture to the milk. Stir quickly just once, then let it settle. The milk will begin to react to the tannins and acidity of the tea and lemon juice, and will curdle the drink. Yes, it will look gross—but this is what you want! Let sit undisturbed at room temperature for 1 hour while it curdles to do its work.

After 1 hour, slowly strain the mixture by running it through a Chemex fitted with a fine coffee filter, or using a fine-mesh strainer fitted with a fine coffee filter and positioned over the top of a bowl or plastic storage container. Don't rush it!

Straining will be a slow, gravity-fed process, as the very fine holes of the coffee filter will only allow a few drips through at a time. You will want to repeat the straining process, using a clean filter each time for two or three passes, until the cocktail is translucent. Two passes will get a decent clarity, but three is better and four will be something to write home about. To speed the straining process, you can use several mason jars and filters, and do it at the same time.

Once the cocktail is preserved with milk and strained, it is shelf stable and can be left at room temperature in a sealed, labeled glass bottle (magic!). The punch will last for 6 months. To serve the drink, shake it over ice, then strain it into an old-fashioned glass and serve it with a cube of fancy ice.

COASTAL
COLLINS

Serves 1

⅓ ounce freshly squeezed lemon
juice (see Notes)

½ ounce Spruce (or Fir) Tip Syrup
(page 53), or preferred syrup

2 ounces vodka, or preferred spirit

3 ounces club soda

Garnish: lemon twist (see Notes) or
a young, feathery spruce tip

12.5% ABV

This drink just tastes like home to us, under the green arbor of the northwestern forests. Our cousins from southeast Alaska first introduced us to the Native American tribes' traditional uses of fir and spruce needles, which are like nature's Gatorade and are consumed raw, brewed in teas, and canned up in jellies each spring in their hometown of Petersburg, Alaska. The new growth tips of both fir and spruce trees hold a delicate citrus flavor, which will surprise and delight you on your first taste. A clean and refreshing vodka collins best allows the spruce flavor to shine through.

Combine the lemon juice, syrup, and vodka in a cocktail shaker and shake over ice until the outside of the shaker is cold, about 15 seconds. Strain into a glass and top with the club soda. Adding the soda now will mix the cocktail without flattening the bubbles. Add 1 cup of fresh ice, or enough to fill the glass to the top. Garnish with a lemon twist or spruce tip, if desired.

NOTES: A collins is a simple cocktail formula to showcase any of your crafted syrups or cordials. Use the same recipe and sub in seasonal syrups and a complementary garnish. If you're using the citrus cordial in the recipe, you may prefer to dial down the lemon juice to ½ ounce.

To make the lemon twist, use a sharp paring knife to remove a 2-inch segment of lemon peel, avoiding the white pith. Squeeze the lemon peel over the top of the glass with a pinch to express the oils, and then drop it in.

198

BLOODY BUNNY

Serves 1

1½ ounces botanical gin or Kale and Chard Vodka (page 101)

3 ounces freshly pressed carrot juice

½ ounce Oleo Saccharum with Herbs (page 58)

½ ounce freshly squeezed lemon juice

1 sprig cilantro (optional)

Tiny pinch of Spicy Herb Garden Salt (page 147), or 1 teaspoon brine from Pickled Carrots (page 153), capers, or green olives

2 teaspoons Pepper Hot Sauce (page 81)

Garnish: Spicy Herb Garden Salt (page 147), baby carrot plus carrot greens

11% ABV

Carrot juice gets no respect, honestly. Except for at a hippie smoothie shop, you just don't see it, and we can't figure out why because it's really very tasty. Especially if you've overwintered your carrots, you need to juice some of the crop you grow. Overwintering is when you let a fall crop of carrots, parsnips, or beets stay in the ground longer than their called-for harvesting date. It is a way to store them in the dirt while also allowing for them to freeze a time or two, which develops more natural sugars and enhances their sweetness. Overwintered carrots are so sweet, their juice is incomparable.

We grow carrots in fall and winter when we can't grow much else and there is room in the beds, so the time frame lines up nicely with Easter. And this cocktail's name, well, it works well with a sinister sense of humor, but we didn't make it up—it's a play on the Bloody Mary. To be honest, we'd probably always choose one of these instead of a Bloody Mary, given the choice. See what you think!

Rim a collins-style or other tall glass with the spicy herb garden salt by placing the salt in a shallow dish, rubbing half of the rim of the glass with a lime or lemon wedge, and then dipping the rim in the salt. Fill the glass with ice. Next, combine the gin, carrot juice, oleo saccharum, lemon juice, cilantro (if using), and spicy herb garden salt or brine over ice in a cocktail shaker and shake for 15 seconds, then fine strain into the rimmed glass. Garnish with carrot greens and a baby carrot.

201

GARDEN GIBSON

Makes 1

2½ ounces Veggie Garden Vodka (page 100), Kale and Chard Vodka (page 101), or London Dry gin

1 teaspoon chive blossom pickling brine (page 158), or more to taste

Garnish: 1 Pickled Chive Blossom (page 158)

33% ABV

The pickled, magenta-colored chive blossom is not only the star of the physical presentation of this cocktail, it also adds a light savoriness with its Technicolor oniony, vinegary brine. Imagine pairing it with a deeply homey and succulent dish like braised beef or oysters on the half shell with a dollop of the same brine. The cocktail is serious, and the purple chive flower (page 158) is memorable. It's going to make an impression at your fancy dinner party, but the ease of preparation may also have you reaching for this recipe on the regular at happy hour.

Chill your glass in the fridge before making this, so the drink is served very cold. For martinis like this one, temperature is as much of an ingredient as anything else. If you're pressed for time, please don't drink a semicold martini. Instead, cheat the chilled-glass effect by adding a scoop of ice to the glass while you mix and shake the drink, then dump that ice before straining the cocktail into the now chilled cup.

Prechill a coupe or a martini glass. Combine the spirit and chive blossom pickling brine in a cocktail shaker with 2 cups of ice. Shake hard for 15 seconds. Strain the cocktail into a chilled martini glass, then add a pickled chive blossom and let it sink to the bottom.

202

ELDERFLOWER SPRITZ

Serves 1

5 fresh mint leaves

2 cucumber slices, one of which should be long and thin for the garnish

⅛ lime wedge

1½ ounces botanical gin or Compound Gin (page 90)

½ ounce Elderflower Liqueur (page 106)

½ ounce Lime Basil Syrup (page 54) or Oleo Saccharum with Herbs (page 58)

5 ounces club soda

8.5% ABV

Light, elegant, and floral, this fizzy cocktail combines most of our favorite things in one tall, icy glass. Picture beads of water running down the side while the bouquet of mint tempts from the top of the glass. Layered in flavor but light and airy, it's begging you to make it by the pitcher and ditch all responsibilities while you sit and watch the light shift and change. The crispness of cucumber meets the refreshment of mint leaves and Lime Basil Syrup (page 54) complements the Elderflower Liqueur (page 106). To say that this cocktail would be perfectly served at a garden party is the understatement of this book.

Prepare a large stemmed wineglass or gin and tonic goblet by filling it to the top with ice and adding three of the mint leaves and the long, thin cucumber slice to the glass, nestled in the ice. Muddle the remaining cucumber slice and lime wedge in a cocktail shaker. Clap the remaining two mint leaves between your hands and add these to the shaker, along with the gin, elderflower liqueur, and syrup. Shake over ice for 10 seconds, then strain into the prepared glass of ice. Top with the club soda and serve with a thin straw to avoid sucking up pieces of herbs.

203

GARDEN PARTY PITCHER

Serves 8

16 cucumber slices, cut into coins

1 lime, cut into 8 wedges

16 fresh mint leaves

12 ounces botanical gin

4 ounces Elderflower Liqueur (page 106)

4 ounces Lime Basil Syrup (page 54) or Oleo Saccharum with Herbs (page 58)

46 ounces club soda

Garnish: handful of fresh mint leaves and vertically sliced pieces of cucumber, cut thinly

Prechill all the ingredients. When ready to serve, prepare a beverage dispenser or pitcher by adding the garnishes—the handful of mint leaves and long slices of cucumber—to the vessel, nestling them in ice. In another pitcher, muddle the cucumber coins and lime wedges. Clap the 16 mint leaves between your hands and add these to the pitcher along with chilled gin, elderflower liqueur, and syrup. Stir. Strain this mixture into the garnished beverage dispenser or pitcher. Top with club soda and stir lightly again. Serve in individual glasses of ice with thin straws to avoid sucking up pieces of herbs.

SPRUCE DROP

Serves 1

1½ ounces citrus or plain vodka

½ ounce Spruce Tip Syrup (page 53)

¾ ounce freshly squeezed lemon juice, squeezed lemon reserved

Garnish: 1 tablespoon Herb Sugar (page 149) or Floral Sugar (page 148)

15% ABV

OTHER COMBINATIONS TO TRY

Vodka + Citrus Cordial (page 59) + freshly squeezed lemon juice + Floral Sugar (page 148)

The lemon drop is like the yoga pants of cocktails. It keeps coming back in style, with each new iteration of it being called something slightly different, but you know what? At the end of the day, it's still comfortable. This one is a little fancy and woodsy because the citrus is complemented by the Spruce Tip Syrup (page 53). Still, you'll recognize it like an old friend. Our favorite cocktails are like that: familiar enough to hit the spot, different enough to be remembered.

Combine the vodka, syrup, and lemon juice in a cocktail shaker and shake over ice until the outside of the shaker is very cold, about 20 seconds. Place the rimming sugar in a shallow dish. Rim a coupe or a martini glass by running the inner side of the squeezed lemon along half of the rim of the glass, then gently dipping it into the sugar. Strain the cocktail into the rimmed glass.

NOTE: Herb Sugar (page 149) on the rim of this cocktail adds a lot. Follow the recipe instructions to make it with fir or spruce tips, where possible, or sub in fresh rosemary.

CROWN JEWEL

Serves 1

2 ripe strawberries (see Notes)

2 ounces London Dry gin, or strawberry-infused gin

1 ounce freshly squeezed orange juice

½ ounce Lime Basil Syrup (page 54)

¼ ounce freshly squeezed lemon juice

2 fresh mint leaves

Garnish: Floral Sugar (page 148) or Herb Sugar (page 149), plus 1 sprig mint and a Candied Citrus Peel (page 136)

18% ABV

Its beautiful presentation will have your friends fawning over this drink, while the 2 ounces of gin make for interesting conversation. If you like a Pimm's Cup, you'll like the Crown Jewel. If you revered strawberry lemonade as the ultimate treat at the rare restaurant outings you went on as a kid, as we did, you'll also be super into this drink, while reliving your childhood.

This drink has only one enemy: winter, when fresh strawberries at the store are looking pretty sad after being picked too early and shipped 1,000 miles. Don't fret, just prepare. Make a strawberry gin (see Notes) when the berries are in season and use it here in place of the fresh muddled strawberries and basic gin.

The name comes from the growing structure of a strawberry plant, which grows from a dense "crown" at the base of the soil. The leaves, fruit, runners, and roots all grow from the crown.

Chill an old-fashioned glass in the fridge, or quick-chill by placing a cup of ice in the glass while you mix the drink. In a cocktail shaker, muddle the berries, then add the gin, orange juice, syrup, and lemon juice. Clap the mint leaves between your hands and drop them in. Shake the cocktail over 1 cup of ice until the outside of the shaker is very cold, about 25 seconds. Place the floral or herb sugar in a shallow dish. Rim the chilled glass in the sugar by running a wedge of lemon along half of the rim of the glass and then dipping it into the mixture. Discard the ice used to chill the glass, then dump (do not strain out the mint pieces or berries) the cocktail into the chilled glass and add ice to fill to the top rim. Garnish with a mint sprig nestled on one side of the ice, and a candied citrus peel resting on the glass rim against the ice. Serve with a straw.

NOTES: One-quarter ounce of Spiced Lime Shrub, aka Ginger Switchel (page 75) will make a tarter drink and add the Pimm's Cup's traditional ginger flavor.

To make the strawberry gin, infuse a bottle of London Dry–style gin with fresh strawberries, washed and sliced, for days. Then strain out the fruit and store the finished gin at room temperature. It will last up to 6 months, with the best flavor and color if consumed within 3.

GREEN GODDESS

Serves 1

2 ounces Kale and Chard Vodka (page 101)

½ ounce freshly squeezed lemon juice

3 drops Herb Tincture (page 86), OR 1 sprig cilantro, 1 fresh mint leaf, and 3 coriander seeds, preferably green

One 2-inch square cube Fancy Ice (page 135)

2 ounces sparkling wine, such as prosecco or brut Champagne

18% ABV

This one will surprise you. It's decidedly less vegetal than you may think—don't let the Kale and Chard Vodka (page 101) intimidate you. You don't even have to love kale salads to enjoy this strangely alluring and beautiful cocktail. When a cilantro plant is going to seed, green coriander seeds grow—this is called bolting, which happens when a plant stops producing new leaf growth and is ending its life cycle. These green coriander seeds are a rare spice to find at stores and such a treat to cook with and add to cocktails. The herbs and lemon bring brightness to the green flavor for this nonsweet cocktail that is perfect for a dinner pairing.

Combine all the ingredients, except the sparkling wine and fancy ice cube, in a cocktail shaker. If using fresh herbs, muddle the herbs and seeds gently in the shaker. Add a scoop of ice to the shaker. Cap and shake for 20 seconds. Fine strain into a coupe glass. Add the ice cube, then the sparkling wine.

ELDERFLOWER VESPER

Serves 1

1 ounce botanical gin or Compound Gin (page 90)

1 ounce vodka

1 ounce Elderflower Liqueur (page 106)

Garnish: 1 lemon twist (see Note)

28.5% ABV

This is the assertive, bossy cousin of the laid-back Elderflower Spritz (page 203). With similar flavors, but served up and booze forward, it's for a different type of night altogether. This one isn't sitting around watching the sun sink lower; it has places to go, and it's going to the dance floor. It's important to stir this cocktail thoroughly so it reaches full dilution for a smooth cocktail. Express the lemon peel over the top of the glass so the fragrant oils add flavor and aroma. It's fun to taste this drink before and after the lemon twist. It's wild how much change simply expressing the oils from the lemon peel brings.

Chill a coupe or martini glass in the fridge, or quick-chill the glass by placing a cup of ice in the glass while you mix the drink. In a cocktail shaker, combine all the ingredients, except the garnish, and shake over ice until the outside of the shaker is very cold, about 20 seconds. Strain the cocktail into the coupe and add the lemon twist.

NOTE: To make the lemon twist, use a sharp paring knife to remove a 2-inch segment of lemon peel, avoiding the white pith. Squeeze the lemon peel over the top of the glass with a pinch to express the oils, and then drop it in.

AMONG THE WILDFLOWERS

Serves 1

2 ounces wheat whiskey, such as Woodinville Straight Rye or Dry Fly Straight Triticale

¾ ounce Lemon Chamomile Shrub (page 73)

1 ounce Hefeweizen beer

Garnish: lemon twist (see Note)

21% ABV

Deceptively simple in its ingredients list, this cocktail uses Lemon Chamomile Shrub (page 73) for an alcohol-forward cocktail that maintains lightness from the floral and citrus flavors. Wheat beer is used, instead of egg whites, to add body and form a light foam on the top, making it a good choice for those with allergies or dietary restrictions to egg.

Chill a coupe glass in the fridge, or quick-chill by placing 1 cup of ice into the glass while you mix the drink. Combine the shrub and beer in a shaker half full of ice and shake for 15 seconds. While measuring, do not overpour the beer or your cocktail will foam too much and want to explode out of the shaker. Remove the ice from the glass. Strain the cocktail into the chilled coupe glass and add the lemon twist.

NOTE: To make a lemon twist, drag a Y-peeler over a washed lemon rind, avoiding cutting in too deep, so that very little white pith is peeled off. Hold this peel over the drink and fold it in half, expressing the oils into the cocktail.

208

WALK IN
THE WOODS

Serves 1

1 ounce bourbon

1 ounce Bellewood Acres apple
brandy, or a brand local to you

1 ounce Fresh-Pressed Apple Cider
(page 114)

¾ ounce freshly squeezed
lemon juice

½ ounce Pumpkin Spice Syrup
(page 62)

Dash of Barkeep's Citrus Bitters
(page 89)

Garnish: nutmeg, apple slice

17% ABV

Apple brandy sounds like something your grandad drinks, but it's worth a revisit from modern drinkers. Brandy distilled from apples maintains a complete smoothness and gentle sweetness you'd expect from the fruit, offset by toasty char flavors added from years of aging in whiskey barrels. The history of cider and brandy making in America is absolutely fascinating, as the two used to be the most prevalent and common alcohols consumed, during a time when our young nation imbibed an estimated THREE times the amount of alcohol that we do today.

The temperance movement, Prohibition, modern farm law and practices, and urban growth have all affected the apple industry significantly, and even more so the growth of cider apples (a more bitter variety than those grown for juice and fruit). The result was that for a long time, we didn't drink very much cider in the USA, and the long tradition of brandy making was upheld by only a few purveyors.

Splitting the liquor between the apple brandy and a higher-proof bourbon, such as Old Grand-Dad (fitting, considering . . .), Maker's Mark 100, or Wild Turkey 101, will give the cocktail more robustness. The apple brandy from Washington State's orchard-to-bottle distillery Bellewood Farms in Lynden, Washington, works beautifully in cocktails and is worth the purchase.

209

Combine all the ingredients, except the garnish, in a shaker with ice, shake for 10 seconds, dump the contents into a rocks glass, and add fresh ice as needed to fill. Fine grate a nutmeg over the top of the glass (or sub ground nutmeg) to taste and rest an apple slice on the rim.

NOTE: Serving a crowd at a harvest or cider-pressing party? Batch this drink ahead of time to make serving a group easy. Mix together all the ingredients, except the nutmeg, a maximum of 4 hours in advance and stir very well. Chill in the fridge and add ¼ ounce of water per serving of cocktail you're making. For example, a batch of 10 cocktails should get 2½ ounces of water added. (The added water will dilute the cocktail properly. Because you will not be shaking them individually with ice, this step is needed.)

MARIONBERRY MOJITO

Serves 1

2 ounces white rum

½ ounce Blackberry and Mint Syrup (page 51)

2 fresh mint leaves

¾ ounce freshly squeezed lime juice

4 ounces club soda

Garnish: 1 sprig mint or Mojito Berries (page 144)

10.5% ABV

A Mojito in the dead heat of summer is one of life's ultimate indulgences, but so many Mojitos at restaurants or bars end up watery, with grainy sugar, or tasting of bruised mint. We'll fix all those problems with this recipe and you won't have to leave home!

We first started using marionberry syrup in our Mojitos at Belinda's mobile bar and now use it at our restaurant, because when colorful ombré purple glasses with big mint garnishes walk by in the hands of a guest, they inspire more cocktail orders. Even better, while the fresh mint leaf is nice to use in summertime, we've found that if you infuse your syrup strongly enough with mint, you can skip the fresh mint and still make Mojitos all year!

To keep the Mojito from overdiluting, fill your glass with fresh ice to chill it. Meanwhile, make sure to use the largest ice cubes you have for shaking in the cocktail shaker. When the shake is complete, before you uncap your shaker, take a second to strain out and discard any water from your chilling ice in the glass and refill it to the very top with fresh ice. Now, strain in your cocktail and top with club soda. We avoid grainy sugar at the bottom of the glass by using a smooth simple syrup instead of muddling in superfine or granulated sugar. To sidestep the bruised, acrid taste that mint can get, this recipe may surprise you by not calling for muddling. Remember, mint is a delicate herb that needs only a clap or a shake to release its fragrant oils. A hard muddle might look cool for your friends, but will not result in a better Mojito. Just say no to the mint muddle!

Combine the rum, syrup, mint leaves, and lime juice in a cocktail shaker and shake with 1 cup of ice until the outside of the shaker is cold, about 15 seconds. Strain into the glass and top with club soda—adding the soda now will mix it without flattening the bubbles. Add 1 cup of ice to the cocktail, or enough to fill the glass to the top. Garnish with a sprig of mint or Mojito Berries.

SOUTHSIDE

Serves 1

3 fresh mint leaves

2 ounces New American or botanical gin, such as the Botanist, Hendrick's, or a locally distilled brand

¾ ounce Blackberry and Mint Syrup (page 51)

¾ ounce freshly squeezed lemon juice

½ ounce freshly squeezed lime juice

Garnish: 1 sprig mint and Mojito Berries (page 144)

18% ABV

There is a time and place for short, alcohol-forward cocktails like this one, and we think the perfect combination is in the garden in the early evening when you're hiding from the expectations of the world. Between the intoxicating smell of your garden's tomato vines and the full 2 ounces of gin in the cocktail, the heart rate lowers and the evening light softens.

This drink has a flavor profile similar to a Mojito, yet its presentation is more similar to a daiquiri. It's a great example of how in cocktails, very small swaps result in highly varying drinks. Swapping a Mojito's lime for lemon, rum for gin, and omitting the club soda creates a different drink experience in the Southside. It should be finished fairly quickly so it doesn't get warm, and so that no one comes and asks you what's for dinner while you're in your happier hour.

Clap the mint leaves between your hands to release the fragrant oils and drop into a cocktail shaker. Add the gin, syrup, lemon and lime juices, and 1 cup of ice and shake until the outside of the shaker is very cold, about 25 seconds. Fine strain into a coupe (to strain out all small ice shards) and garnish with a sprig of mint and Mojito Berries on a toothpick, resting on the rim of the glass.

213

SMASH

Serves 1

3 to 4 fresh berries—some combination of blackberries, raspberries, and strawberries

1 sprig thyme

2 ounces rye whiskey

¾ ounce freshly squeezed lemon juice

½ ounce Blackberry and Mint Syrup (page 51) or Strawberry Syrup (page 50)

3 drops Herb Tincture (page 86; optional)

Garnish: 1 sprig fresh mint

23% ABV

Muddling fresh thyme and berries into a cocktail is entirely satisfying, a bit like a workout followed by a sauna, except with near instant gratification. You work hard for a minute, and then get nice and melty, limbs loosening afterward as you settle into the drink.

Take note that the hard muddle works here because thyme is a woody herb with sturdy leaves that can stand up to the abuse, as opposed to delicate herbs like mint, which are prone to releasing an off-putting, acrid flavor if faced with the same tool.

Venise would sub in gin for the rye whiskey, and Belinda would say that's fine, but choose a London Dry gin, something bold enough to hold up against the fruity sweetness as the spice of the rye whiskey does. You should serve a Smash with the whole fruit bits in the glass for texture and color, so add a straw for the sake of your teeth's appearance.

Muddle the fresh berries and a sprig of thyme at the bottom of a cocktail shaker. Add the whiskey, lemon juice, and syrup. Add 1 cup of ice and shake for 10 seconds. Dump the mixture into an old-fashioned glass and add ice to fill the glass, if needed. Serve with a straw and garnish with a sprig of fresh mint.

215

MIDNIGHT AT THE MOVIES

Serves 1

2 ounces Cherry Whiskey (page 95)

5 ounces Classic Coke, preferably Mexican Coke (made with real cane sugar, sold in a glass bottle)

Handful of shelled salted peanuts (optional)

Garnish: 2 Whiskey-Soaked Cherries (page 95)

11% ABV

Deceptively simple and entirely nostalgic, this is a cocktail we've had many guests profess to be the best drink of their life at our Soda Shop bar and tasting room. Memories are a powerful taste enhancer, and most Americans have a fond summer childhood memory with an ice-cold cherry Coke.

Southerners know what we're talking about when we tell you that it isn't a bad idea to add a handful of peanuts to the bottom of this cocktail for a shock of unexpected saltiness to a sweet beverage, and a delicious cola-coated peanut snack after you finish your drink.

Fill a collins glass full of ice. Add the cherry whiskey, top with Coke, and stir a few times. Optional: Add a handful of peanuts to the bottom of the glass. Garnish with whiskey-soaked cherries on a toothpick.

CUCUMBER BASIL GIMLET

Serves 1

2 ounces gin of choice

½ ounce Lime Basil Syrup (page 54)

½ ounce freshly squeezed lime juice

1 ounce fresh cucumber juice

Garnish: We got extra with this one: borage, chamomile, calendula, basil, and a cucumber slice are pictured here.

17% ABV

A gimlet was Belinda's go-to bar order in her twenties; unique enough to stand out, yet simple enough that most bars had the ingredients to make it. The combination of gin, lime juice, and sugar is widely accessible, but the recipe isn't super well known, so it may just surprise you and become a new favorite.

This very simple and delicious drink makes a perfect backdrop for your garden to show off whatever is growing at the moment, like the borderline excessive garnishes we added here, Buzz Button Gin (page 92) that will give a buzzy sensation and cucumber juice for added freshness. Further invention can come from whether you serve your gimlet in a stemmed glass "up" (shaken with ice but served without) as you may receive if you order a gimlet in a craft cocktail bar, or in a pint glass over ice, as in the recipe as follows, plus a splash of club soda, which is how I often receive it at restaurants. Part of the fun of the drink is the many forms in which we've enjoyed it.

Up for some extra fun? Split the alcohol between 1 ounce of gin and 1 ounce of Buzz Button Gin (page 92) to add some pizzazz.

Combine all the ingredients, except the garnishes, in a cocktail shaker and shake over 2 cups of ice until the outside of the shaker is very cold, about 25 seconds. Strain into a martini glass. Garnish. We recommend an edible flower with an herb sprig and a cucumber slice.

THE DASHING GENTLEMAN

Serves 1

¼ ounce sweet vermouth

1 ounce maraschino liqueur

2 ounces Cherry Whiskey (page 95)

2 dashes Barkeep's Citrus Bitters (page 89)

Vanilla Sugar (page 149; optional)

Garnish: 1 Whiskey-Soaked Cherry (page 95), orange twist (see Note)

28% ABV

This drink is Manhattan-reminiscent for the brown spirit lovers, but ends up tasting—and please forgive us if this doesn't immediately transport you to your childhood—as if you got to the end of a cherry Tootsie Roll Pop and got impatient enough to bite through the remainder of the hard candy into the chocolaty center. Or, in less colorful terms, it tastes as if you muddled the cherry into a Manhattan, if that cherry was fresh from the orchard instead of one of the supersweet, lye-soaked, red-dyed maraschino cherries that are traditional to the cocktail. But really think about it when you first taste this—we know you'll instantly remember that Tootsie Roll lollipop!

Rinse a coupe glass with the sweet vermouth by pouring it into the glass and swirling it all around to coat the glass, then discard any remaining liquid.

Prepare the cocktail: Combine the maraschino liqueur, cherry whiskey, and bitters, plus 1 cup of ice in a mixing glass. Stir smoothly with a barspoon at least 10 times to chill and dilute the cocktail.

If using the vanilla sugar, place it in a shallow dish. Rim just half of the glass with vanilla sugar by running a thread of bourbon along half of the glass rim with your finger or a pastry brush, then dipping the rim into the vanilla sugar.

Strain the drink into the prepared coupe glass.

Garnish with a whiskey-soaked cherry on a toothpick and an orange twist.

NOTE: Use a sharp paring knife to remove a 2-inch segment of orange peel, avoiding the white pith. Squeeze the orange peel over the top of the glass with a pinch to express the oils, and then drop it in.

BACK PORCH LEMONADE

Serves 1

1 fresh basil leaf

1 ounce vodka or gin of choice

½ ounce Foraged Elderflower
Cordial (page 61)

1 ounce freshly squeezed lemon juice

½ ounce Lime Basil Syrup (page 54)

2 ounces club soda

Garnish: 1 sprig basil

8.5 % ABV

Mix up one of Venise's favorite cocktails of all time. The crushed ice matters, because the extra dilution from the fast-melting pebbled or crushed ice makes the drink go down extra-smooth. If you don't have a crushed ice machine, fill a sealable bag with large ice cubes, push out the air, wrap the bag with a towel, and beat it with a mallet or rolling pin until the ice is crushed—it's every bit worth the effort. Plus, it's kind of satisfying.

Clap the basil leaf between your hands before placing it in a cocktail shaker with the vodka, cordial, lemon juice, and syrup. Cap and shake for 20 seconds. Serve over crushed ice in a tall glass. Top with the club soda, garnish with a basil sprig, and serve with a straw.

PITCHER PUNCH

Serves 12

12 ounces (1½ cups) Berry Liqueur (page 105), or sub in seltzer water for the nonalcoholic version

12 ounces (1½ cups) Strawberry Syrup (page 50) or Oleo Saccharum with Herbs (page 58)

Optional: 12 drops Herb Tincture (page 86) or Barkeep's Citrus Bitters (page 89)

6 ounces still water

12 ounces (1½ cups) freshly squeezed lemon juice

36 ounces club soda or three 12-ounce cans seltzer water

Garnish: berries and fresh herbs

6% ABV

Simple things are best: everyone needs their favorite white T-shirt, a go-to road trip playlist, and this recipe in their back pocket for whenever hosting duties pop up. It's got a 95 percent success rate in likeability for a crowd, it's low alcohol content for afternoon parties, simple to prepare, and keeps well in a beverage dispenser or pitcher so guests can serve one themselves. Just don't forget to put out an alcohol-free version as well, and label them clearly!

To make this punch totally nonalcoholic, replace the liquor with additional seltzer water and consider adding five or six drops of Herb Tincture (page 86), Distilled Floral Water (page 127), or Barkeep's Citrus Bitters (page 89) to add balance and intrigue.

Pregarnishing glasses is a nice signal to guests that all they have to do is add ice and pour their drink.

Combine the liqueur, syrup, herb tincture (if using), water, and lemon juice in a gallon-size drink dispenser and chill in the fridge. Just before serving, fill the dispenser with ice and add the club soda or seltzer water. Set out ice cubes, cups, and garnishes for guests to serve themselves.

NOTE: As the host, you set the tone for alcohol consumption at a party, and a big signal you give to guests on how much to consume is how big the glasses are. Bartenders typically fill cups to the top with ice for a properly chilled drink that won't dilute quickly. Most people don't, plus they pour the drink to the top, thereby unwittingly serving themselves a few extra ounces with every glass. Use small sherry glasses, wine flutes, teacups, or pint-size jelly jars to control your guests' pour size, so everyone can have multiple glasses without overindulging.

BLOODY MARY

Serves 1

6 ounces Bloody Mary Mix

2 ounces Veggie Garden Vodka
(page 100)

Garnish: Spicy Herb Garden Salt
(page 147) for rim, Quick-Pickled
Green Beans (page 152), 1 fresh
celery rib with the leaves intact, and
1 Bloody Mary Skewer (page 140)

13% ABV

Once, when Belinda was bartending for a wedding from her 1967 canned ham trailer, she was asked for a Bloody Mary. It wasn't on the bride and groom's menu for the evening, and when Belinda had to tell her no, the lady turned and walked away from the bar drinkless. This is how people feel about Bloody Marys, we've generally found: die-hard, or no, thanks. Bloody Mary or nothing!

We were in the "no, thanks" camp until we learned that what we actually didn't like about the drink was the canned tomato juice and horseradish. So, this recipe uses neither and now we're crazy about it. Fresh tomato juice is delicious and nothing at all like canned, and the heat of this recipe comes from Poblano Liqueur (page 99). If you don't want to add the extra step, add a teaspoon of Pepper Tincture (page 87), grate in some fresh horseradish, or blend in a few slices of jalapeño.

Place the rimming salt in a shallow dish. Using a wedge of lemon and gently dipping the glass into the salt, rim half of the rim of a pint glass with the salt. Gently tap off any excess and fill the pint glass with ice. Add the Bloody Mary mix, followed by the vodka, and stir. In one corner of the glass, stand up a few pickled green beans and a celery stick with the leaves intact. Rest a Bloody Mary skewer over the rim and serve.

222

BLOODY MARY MIX

Makes about 80 ounces, enough for 12 Bloody Mary cocktails

60 ounces (5 cups) fresh tomato juice, from about 6 pounds tomatoes, any large fruit variety (but avoid paste varieties like Roma, which have less juice) run through a juicer (see page 117)

8 ounces celery juice, from whole pieces and leaves run through a juicer

4 ounces freshly squeezed lemon juice

1 whole, large tomato

2 garlic cloves, chopped finely

4 ounces Worcestershire sauce

1 ounce Poblano Liqueur (page 99), or substitute 4 teaspoons horseradish, if you insist

1 teaspoon balsamic vinegar

1 teaspoon salt, or to taste

1 teaspoon celery salt, or to taste

1 teaspoon paprika

½ teaspoon ground cumin

½ teaspoon ground coriander

¼ teaspoon cayenne pepper

8 dashes Pepper Hot Sauce (page 81) or to taste

Combine all the ingredients in a blender (or use a bowl and an immersion blender). Puree until smooth, then store in glass bottles with a lid in the fridge. This mixture lasts for 3 days, or can be pressure canned or frozen and defrosted when you're ready to serve it.

VERDE MARIA

Serves 6

8 ounces tequila

4 ounces Jalapeño Tequila
(page 96), or omit and use
12 ounces tequila plus
½ jalapeño, blended

2 ounces Poblano Liqueur
(page 99; optional)

16 ounces tomatillo juice (green
tomato juice can work, if needed)

3 ounces poblano juice

3 ounces cucumber juice

3 ounces celery juice

3 ounces freshly squeezed lime juice

½ teaspoon salt

½ teaspoon celery salt

½ teaspoon piment d'Espelette or
mild chili powder

Garnish: Spicy Herb Garden Salt
(page 147); cucumber, sliced thinly
lengthwise; cilantro sprigs; and
3 cherry tomatoes per garnish,
speared on a toothpick

12% ABV

We never met a salsa verde we didn't like, and these are essentially that, in drink form. Even if you've never been a huge fan of Bloody Marys, you may find yourself ready to drink a pitcher of Verde Marias: they're a different beast entirely. This recipe is a great way to use up green tomatoes in your garden if you're nearing the end of the season and don't see them ripening, or if a wind has knocked them off the plants. When we grow tomatillos in our garden, or even when we don't (they will come back year after year if you let them and love to grow in a compost pile), they have a way of going crazy and ripening all their fruit at once, and we use that as an excuse to blend up this mixture.

Want to make it hotter? Add a few drops of Pepper Tincture (page 87).

Combine the tequila, jalapeño tequila, poblano liqueur, all the juices, the salt, celery salt, and piment d'Espelette in a pitcher or blender and pulse or stir. Chill the entire mixture until just before serving. Place the rimming salt in a shallow dish, then rim tall glasses by running a lime wedge along half of the rim of each glass and gently dipping it into the salt. Fill the glasses very full of ice, garnished with a long slice of cucumber standing up in each glass at one end, alongside a sprig of cilantro. Hold these in place with a toothpick of cherry tomatoes.

MICHELADA

Serves 1

4 ounces Bloody Mary Mix
(page 222), chilled

10 ounces preferred Mexican beer,
such as Corona, Tecate, or Modelo

Garnish: lime wedges and Spicy
Herb Garden Salt (page 147)
for the rim

7% ABV

Belinda once almost died of an epic hangover in a little town in Tuscany at 18 years old, but she discovered that standing still in the villa's pool holding a red beer were the only things keeping her in the land of the living. While that sentence is filled with hyperbole, the Michelada really came through at the time, and this superfresh upgrade is a must-try, no exaggeration needed.

Chill a pint glass in the freezer for 15 minutes or more before making this drink. Place the rimming salt in a shallow dish, then rim the glass by running a lime wedge along half of the rim and gently dipping it into the salt. Add the cold Bloody Mary mix to the rimmed glass, then slowly pour in the beer. Garnish with a lime wedge.

SEATTLE SLING

Serves 1

¾ ounce freshly squeezed
lemon juice

½ ounce Lavender Honey Syrup
(page 57)

2 ounces botanical gin or
Compound Gin (page 90)

1 ounce vermouth bianco

2 ounces club soda

Garnish: fresh sage leaves and a
lavender sprig, Candied Citrus Peel
(page 136)

14% ABV

This is a cocktail for those long summers that stretch into fall, when the nights turn cool but the days of sunshine stretch on until October some years, making people sweat into their pumpkin spice lattes. We just can't transition to those full-fledged fall flavors when it still feels like summer outside. So, we find ourselves making drinks like this one, which toe the line between seasons. It can be made sweeter if your taste buds are asking for that, though this drink originated as a more interesting version of a gin and soda or vodka soda—approachable and clean.

It's also a recipe that is just as lovely without the booze; if you choose, simply leave it out and replace it with a few drops of Barkeep's Citrus Bitters (page 89) and an additional splash of club soda. Lavender and sage are both calming, cleansing herbs that have strong aromatic powers to help you breathe easier, slow down, and enjoy the lingering warmth of late summer. The drink tastes complex and nuanced, far beyond your average mocktail.

Combine all the ingredients, except the club soda and garnishes, in a cocktail shaker with 1 cup of ice and shake. Strain the cocktail into a glass filled with 1 cup of fresh ice and top with the club soda. Garnish with fresh herbs and a candied citrus peel.

227

COCK'S CROW

Serves 1

1 ounce blanco tequila

½ ounce Jalapeño Tequila (page 96)

2 ounces freshly squeezed
grapefruit juice

¾ ounce freshly squeezed lime juice

½ ounce Citrus Cordial (page 59)

1½ ounces wheat beer

Tiny pinch of kosher salt

Garnish: raspberries, fresh sage leaf

10% ABV

Mix up one of these spicy, tart, and irresistibly salty drinks for a great brunch cocktail that riffs on the Paloma. While margaritas get the glory here, stateside, the Paloma is the national drink of Mexico. It can be made with grapefruit soda, but this version uses fresh juice for a brighter drink and cordial for sweetness. Grapefruit and tequila both blend nicely with a wide variety of flavors, so change out the syrup flavor if you'd like.

The Cock's Crow is intended to pair with food and is particularly nice with brunch (huevos rancheros or a bacon breakfast sandwich are asking nicely to be served with one). The color of an early sunrise, this drink is more sassy than sweet, hence the rooster's crow reference. As in the Among the Wildflowers cocktail (page 208), beer is used here to add body and create a vegan-friendly foam. If you don't have time to infuse the Jalapeño Tequila (page 96), you can use a full ounce and a half of the blanco tequila plus a few drops of Pepper Tincture (page 87).

This is a great example of how cocktails evolve with just a change or two in the ingredients and proportions. Omit the beer and replace it with club soda, and it's a more classic Paloma. To make it a Salty Dog, sub vodka for the tequila and omit the syrup. Then, if you remove the salt, it's a Greyhound. But make it as written below? Well, there's nothing else to call that but a Cock's Crow. It's a sassy kind of wake-up with a blush sunrise color.

Combine the tequilas, juices, cordial, and beer in a cocktail shaker with a pinch of salt. Shake over ice with hard, firm shakes for about 30 seconds. Beer will expand quickly and foam in the cocktail shaker, so take care while uncapping. Strain into a tall glass filled with crushed ice. Garnish with raspberries and a sage leaf on a toothpick.

APPLE BETTY MARTINI

Serves 1

Lemon wedge

Vanilla Sugar (page 149)

¾ ounce Brown Butter Vodka (page 107)

¾ ounce bourbon

1 ounce Fresh-Pressed Apple Cider (page 114)

1 teaspoon Apple Butter (page 66)

Garnish: apple fan (see Note)

15% ABV

Our maternal grandmother, Nanny, had this dessert in her repertoire that was like an apple crisp but entirely, 100 percent better, and it was called Apple Betty. This drink is my homage to that dessert in all its buttery, apple, and cinnamon goodness. Serve it after dinner as a nightcap.

Rim a chilled coupe glass with vanilla sugar by placing the vanilla sugar in a shallow plate, running a wedge of lemon along the rim of half of the glass, and then dipping it into the sugar. Combine all the other ingredients, except the garnish, in a cocktail shaker with ice and shake for 20 seconds. Fine strain the cocktail into your sugared glass. Garnish with an apple fan.

NOTE: To make an apple fan, slice an apple thinly, then stack the slices together at one end and spear them through with a toothpick. Rest the toothpick on the side of the glass so the apples are fanned and the tips stand up in the glass.

BONFIRE

Serves 1

2 ounces hard cider

1 ounce Laird's applejack, or local apple brandy

½ ounce Scotch, such as Dewar's

1 ounce Onyx Oxymel (page 78)

¾ ounce red wine float—choose a sweeter, fruity red wine, such as Shiraz

Garnish: star anise

14.5% ABV

This cocktail riffs on a New York sour. With a beautifully layered appearance, it is like gazing into an autumn bonfire, one of our favorite family pastimes, especially when the workday is done and a cocktail is involved. You usually need a sweet and a sour component for this drink—generally lemon juice and honey syrup—but instead, we save you time and energy by using the ever-helpful Onyx Oxymel (page 78)—a honey and vinegar shrub that covers both at once.

Combine the cider, applejack, Scotch, and oxymel in a cocktail shaker with 1 cup of ice. Shake for 15 seconds, then strain into a tall collins glass full of fresh ice. Using a barspoon, float the red wine by pouring it very slowly over the back of the spoon so it sits briefly on top before it sinks slowly. Garnish with star anise.

HOMECOMING MARGARITA

Serves 1

¼ orange

1 ounce tequila

½ ounce mezcal

½ ounce Cointreau or other orange liqueur

1 ounce Pumpkin Spice Syrup (page 62)

1 ounce freshly squeezed lime juice

A few dashes of Pepper Tincture (page 87; optional)

Garnish: Vanilla Sugar (page 149; optional), marigold flowers, 1 jalapeño speared with a toothpick

15% ABV

Cempasúchil is the Aztec name of the marigold, a flower native to Mexico that should be planted in every cocktail garden. The strong color, scent, and companion-planting benefits of the flower earn its place in your garden. It's also one of the last flowers still blooming in the fall, so we love it in this margarita, which feels like a transitional drink for the changing season with its light smokiness and heat.

The pungent scent of the leaves and flowers were believed by the Aztecs to call the deceased back to their loved ones. It is tradition for marigolds to be heaped, strung, and bunched in cemeteries as brilliantly colored *ofrendas* (scented offerings) to honor deceased loved ones on Dios de Los Muertos. The ofrendas often have the flowers alongside tequila and mezcal, as in this cocktail. Pumpkin Spice Syrup (page 62) is a nod to the squash that ripens at the same time of year, and the cinnamon and nutmeg in the syrup offset the mezcal well.

Place orange quarter in a cocktail shaker and muddle strongly to break up the fruit, releasing the juice and the oils in the orange rind. Add the tequila, mezcal, Cointreau, syrup, lime juice, and pepper tincture (if using). Add ice and shake vigorously for 20 seconds. If rimming with vanilla sugar, place the vanilla sugar in a shallow dish, rub the inside of the orange along the rim of half of a glass, and dip the edge into the sugar. Fill the glass with fresh ice. Fine strain the cocktail into your sugared glass. Garnish with marigold flowers tucked to one side of the glass plus a speared jalapeño.

231

NANCY'S WHISKEY SOUR

Serves 1

2 ounces whiskey (the Nanc prefers 100% rye)

¾ ounce freshly squeezed lemon juice

¾ ounce preferred syrup (the Nanc prefers Lavender Honey, page 48)

½ ounce (or about 1 large) egg white, or substitute aquafaba (chickpea liquid) as a vegan/allergy-friendly alternative

1 ounce club soda

Garnish: 3 drops Barkeep's Citrus Bitters (page 89) or something aromatic, such as a sprig of lavender or other fresh herb to complement your chosen syrup

18% ABV

If you drink three or four of these one night with your cousins and 86-year-old grandmother while staying in a tiny home nestled in a cherry orchard east of the mountains, you will have a very silly time and wake up with the sides of your mouth sore and chapped from the astringency of the lemon. Do it anyway.

Our annual Granddaughter–Grandma Nancy trips take up just three days of our year, but build some of our most lasting memories. It's difficult to try to sum up the treasure that is our grandmother, but suffice it to say they got it wrong and the phrases should be "She's a good-time Nancy" and "what a negative Sally." Our grandma, referred to often as "the Nanc" is the world's reigning queen of happy hour, but it isn't just that her drinks are good (they are), or the snacks plentiful and displayed nicely (they also are), it's that the woman is a champion conversationalist. The Nanc is the rare combination of person who is just as good a listener as she is talker, and it's no surprise that this has led to an abundance of friends. She has taught us to listen more than we talk (we're still learning that one), slow down at the end of each day for a little ritual with yourself, and don't let it be a big deal to invite people over—do it frequently and without too much thought. After all, it's just a drink. This cocktail is her favorite for Belinda to make for her. She's declared it "yummers" on every occasion it's been served to her.

A true sour, made with egg white for a silky texture, is an impressive cocktail to show off your home bartending skills, but actually quite easy to make once you know the technique. Don't let anyone know how easy, and you can keep impressing them time and time again. (However, these are not the drinks to choose for a dinner party, unless you're looking for an arm workout during your hosting duties.) Through an intense and multistep shake, the egg white will wrap the alcohol in a silky, velvet texture that makes for the smoothest cocktail. Or you can use aquafaba (the liquid left in a can of chickpeas) as a good vegan- or allergy-friendly substitute that is practically tasteless, clear, and whips up similar to egg whites.

The vessel the drink is served in plays a big role in its success. A stemmed coupe (like the one pictured) or a large martini glass not only look the prettiest—and this cocktail is big on presentation—they help keep the drink cold. The key is a wide opening of the cup for the foam to sit and distribute the aroma of citrus and spirit. A fresh garnish that complements the ingredients can further draw you in.

RECIPE CONTINUES

232

In a cocktail shaker, combine all the ingredients, except the club soda and garnish. Firmly cap the shaker and do a dry shake for 1 minute (it's a workout!). Shake vigorously to create maximum "action" of the ingredients against the walls of the shaker. This "dry shake" technique will help break up the proteins of the egg white or aquafaba to create a foam. This cocktail is all about texture. Gently, so as not to kill the foam, add a big scoop of ice to the shaker and then shake vigorously for another 30 seconds.

Strain the drink into a coupe or stemmed wineglass. Some foam will come through and settle on the top. Capture the extra foam that has clung to the sides of the shaker by "rinsing" the shaker with the club soda, swirling it to catch the foam, and then straining it on the top of the drink. If done correctly, there will be a solid line of silky foam ½ inch thick at the top of the glass and a bright, transparent liquid layer of cocktail below. Garnish with Barkeep's Citrus Bitters or a sprig of lavender or other fresh herb laid across the foam.

Important Nancy serving suggestion: Serve the cocktail with a side of crackers, meats, cheese, popcorn, and mixed nuts, or whatever you have on hand. Use whatever partial bags of them that you have in the pantry, so long as you put them on something pretty. Really, we mean any very random and unmatching assortment—it doesn't matter, because the drinks are great and the company is even better. Invite over the first person you think of who will say yes, and when you're done, take at least 30 minutes to say good-bye.

234

HOME FOR THE HOLIDAYS ON THE RANCH (TO FIND LOVE)

Serves 1

2 ounces bourbon

¾ ounce freshly squeezed lemon juice

1 teaspoon Apple Butter (page 66)

1 tablespoon Pumpkin Spice Syrup (page 62)

1 egg white, or substitute 1 ounce aquafaba (chickpea liquid) for an allergy-friendly alternative

Garnish: 3 drops Barkeep's Citrus Bitters (page 89)

19% ABV

Each winter, we transform our Soda Shop into a nostalgic winter wonderland with a holiday menu and decor that evokes a cozy cabin, complete with a Christmas tree farm on our bar's patio. It's a silly tradition we added to make the holiday drinks' names as fun to say as possible. This sour tastes like a plucky leading lady's drink order in a Hallmark Christmas movie, right before she catches eyes with her true love across the small-town bar's dance floor.

Follow the Nancy's Whiskey Sour cocktail instructions (page 232), but use apple butter and pumpkin spice syrup for the sweetener. When the cocktail has been strained into the glass and 1 cup of ice added, add a scent to the white foam top by garnishing with bitters. Using a dropper, add 3 drops of the citrus bitters on top of the foam, and using a toothpick, swipe up on each from the center to make a heart. Use the toothpick to connect the hearts through the center, with one sweeping line.

235

PLENTY GOOD

Serves 1

1 ounce Fennelcello (page 109)

1 ounce Bailey's Irish Cream

Optional: sugar-coated fennel candy (see Notes) or a Fennel Pollen Salt (page 148) rim

15.5 % ABV

Venise's favorite oddball candy as a child was the chewy, hard-shelled, pink and white capsulelike candies Good & Plenty. Most seven-year-olds aren't wild about licorice flavors but she was, so Belinda, being the great sister she is, made this cocktail to bring her back to that nostalgic time. It can be either a shot or served as a highball with club soda. It's an example of how to use Fennelcello (page 109) in an aggressively fennel cocktail, whereas Roman's Empire (page 192) is more subtle.

Chocolate-covered licorice is a popular dessert in Scandinavian countries, and if you like those flavors, you've got to try this drink. You can layer it for ultimate visual effect by pouring it carefully over the back of a barspoon to slow the flow and pouring in order of density. Heavier ingredients will stay at the bottom, while lighter density ingredients will float on top.

Prechill your liqueurs. Layer the shot by first pouring Fennelcello into a chilled shot glass. Shake the Bailey's hard with ice in a cocktail shaker for 15 seconds, aiming to get some frothiness. Strain it slowly into the shot glass, holding the shaker in one hand and a barspooon upside down in the other, pouring the Bailey's so it runs down the back of the spoon slowly before hitting the Fennelcello. Frothing the Bailey's through shaking and pouring it this way will help hold your layers.

NOTES: *Mukhwas* (sugar-covered fennel candy, which look just like rainbow jimmies sprinkles but taste so much better) is available from South Asian grocers and online, and makes a fun, colorful rim for this shot. To rim the glass, place the candy in a shallow dish, coat half of the rim of a shot glass with honey, and then dip it into the fennel candy.

Alternatively, if you're like Venise and enjoy salty-sweet combinations immensely, use Fennel Pollen Salt (page 148) to rim the shot glass.

PUMPKIN SPICE ESPRESSO MARTINI

Serves 1

1½ ounces vodka or Brown Butter Vodka (page 107)

¾ ounce Pumpkin Spice Syrup (page 62)

½ ounce half-and-half

1 ounce prepared espresso or cold brew coffee, chilled

Garnish: 3 coffee beans

13.5% ABV

Mixed up with or without a shot of espresso, the Pumpkin Spice Martini is perfect for pre–going out drinks with friends, family game nights, book club get-togethers, and celebratory toasting moments with your crowd gathered around a warm table. You can adapt this drink to use bourbon, if you prefer a stronger perspective from the spirit. Here, it calls for vodka, which lets the pumpkin flavor shine.

This is an excellent candidate for a prebatched multiserving cocktail. Because of the stability of the cream and syrup ingredients, it will sit well in the fridge after you measure out the ingredients and still taste good hours later. However, to get the creamy, frothy texture and dilute the cocktail, you will need to shake each one in a cocktail shaker with ice just before serving.

Combine the vodka, syrup, half-and-half, and espresso in a cocktail shaker. Cap and dry shake, hard, for 20 seconds to build a foam. Add ice and shake again for 30 more seconds to continue building foam while chilling and diluting the drink. Strain the cocktail into a chilled coupe. Garnish with three coffee beans.

237

SPARKLER

Serves 1

½ ounce any preferred syrup (Cranberry Rosemary, page 65, is pictured here)

½ ounce cranberry juice, Fresh-Pressed Apple Cider (page 114), or 3 dashes Barkeep's Citrus Bitters (page 89)

4 ounces sparkling wine, chilled

Garnish: 1 sprig rosemary or whole berries

9% ABV

Christmas brunch with our dad's side of the family is a laid-back affair, with a buffet we come back to for multiple plates over the slow-paced hours of gifting and catching up since we last saw each other (likely only a week before, or honestly, maybe even the night before—we're close like that!). The buffet is always, blessedly, the same. It's made up of premade egg strata casseroles, sweet breads and rolls, a never-ending coffee pot for our family of Nordic guzzlers, and a sparkling wine bar. The juices are cranberry, orange, and grapefruit, and now that we're grown and have introduced them, an array of homemade syrups to pair with the juices.

Let sparkling wine chill in a bucket of ice next to a row of flutes and a few options of syrups—your Christmas morning, wedding shower, New Year's Eve party, or Thanksgiving dinner just got easier on the host and a whole lot more delicious! The self-serve Sparkler cocktail bar is impossible to mess up, and serving it this way gives guests at a shower or party something to do while you take coats or eat an appetizer.

Combine the syrup and juice in a Champagne flute. Add the sparkling wine, pouring very slowly as the bubbles will fizz when exposed to acidity from the syrup or juice. We, of course, prefer freshly squeezed juice, but take note: fresh juice fizzes up considerably more than store-bought, so pour extra slowly! Drop a rosemary sprig or berry to the bottom for texture and extra color.

239

HARVEST MOON PUNCH

Serves 16

Punch

2 cups Fresh-Pressed Apple Cider
(page 114)

½ cup Cranberry Rosemary
Syrup (page 65) or preferred syrup
(suggestions follow)

8 to 10 dashes Barkeep's Citrus
Bitters (page 89)

¼ teaspoon fine sea salt

4 cups gin of choice

1 cup sparkling wine

1½ cups water or club soda to
mingle flavors and mellow the taste

Ice Mold

Bottled distilled water to
fill container

Garnishes, such as cinnamon
sticks, star anise, whole cranberries,
sage leaves, dried Citrus Wheels
(page 138), or colorfast edible
flowers (see page 35)

18% ABV

Serving punch is a no-brainer for hosting a crowd: pour it all in a bowl and get back to the party! We are big believers in making parties fun for both the guests and ourselves, which is why we often turn to punch.

Punch got a bad rep for a lot of years due to those Technicolor, supersweet, melting ice cream punches enjoyed at baby showers and church picnics. But don't you also remember enjoying them? Punch was never a bad thing, it just went out of style for a while, and it deserves an update. Everything old is new again eventually, and whether you serve it as Belinda does in an antique punch bowl or in a glass self-serve beverage dispenser, at the end of the day, punch is just a reliable recipe for serving big groups. Easy is important to us, or we might never have people over.

To make the decorative ice, which is by no means required but nice for fancier occasions, use recycled containers or kitchen bowls, Bundt pans for an ice mold, anything that will fit in your punch bowl or dispenser and fits in your freezer. Milk cartons cut down to about 5 inches high, gallon ice cream pails filled just 4 inches high with water, and Bundt cake pans all work. Your goal is a large hunk of ice so the ice melts slowly. Using an interestingly shaped mold is extra attractive.

Put out appropriately sized cups when serving punch. A serving is about 4½ ounces and fits well in a teacup, coupe, or martini glass. This is why the decorative cups in punch bowl sets are always so small! Eight-ounce jelly jars filled with ice also work nicely.

MAKE THE PUNCH

Combine all the ingredients, except the water or club soda, in your punch bowl or dispenser and chill.

MAKE THE ICE

Fill your ice mold container halfway with bottled distilled water. Add your choice of garnishes to the container, then put it in the freezer and freeze until mostly solid. This will hold in your garnishes and prevent them from floating. (If you skip this step and do a single freeze, that's fine—your decorations will just end up in the punch more quickly if they're not submerged in a layer of ice.) Next, fill the form to the top with more distilled water. Freeze again. Before serving, remove the ice from the form by running the side and bottom of the form quickly under hot tap water.

TO SERVE

Just before the party begins, add the ice block and club soda. Avoid stirring the punch after this point or the bubbles will flatten.

NOTE: You may substitute lime-flavored seltzer in this recipe to lower the alcohol content to 15% ABV and make the punch more affordable.

HOT TODDY

Serves 1

4 ounces water

1 tea bag (optional)

2 ounces bourbon or whiskey

¾ ounce your choice of syrup

1 slice lemon or other citrus

Garnish: cinnamon stick,
chamomile flower, or Citrus Wheel
(page 138)—see Garnishing Tip

11% ABV

---

*OTHER COMBINATIONS
TO TRY*

Pumpkin Spice Syrup (page 62)
+ chai + freshly squeezed lemon
juice + whiskey

Oleo Saccharum with
Herbs (page 58) + freshly
squeezed Meyer lemon juice
(no tea) + whiskey

Lavender Honey Syrup (page 57)
+ freshly squeezed blood orange
juice + dried chamomile flower
tea (see page 125) + whiskey

A hot toddy is our comfort cocktail, the one our paternal Grandma Nancy (you remember, the Nanc from page 232) has always directed us to mix up at the first sign of a throat tickle. We don't wait until the verge of an illness to make one, but instead we eagerly await the first nights in fall when the air is chilled enough after sunset to make a fire in the farm's outdoor kitchen stove. We can sit near it with our hands wrapped around a steaming mug of a hot toddy and melt a little into the physical and metaphorical warmth of this drink.

The formula for a hot toddy cocktail is simple. The base of lemon, hot water, sugar or honey, and whiskey is a great soother of throats and cabin fever. Make in the fall with simple syrups in delightfully cozy flavors like apple cider and cinnamon or chai. In winter, when the stores fill with such fresh citrus as blood oranges, tangelos, and Meyer lemons, we love to try the subtle differences by mixing up the citrus in toddies. In recent years, we began ordering oranges shipped directly from the Northern California family farm Papa's Citrus and it was like tasting an orange for the first time, so bright and sweet was the freshly picked fruit to our northern tongues.

Heat the water, in a saucepot or kettle, to very warm but not boiling. Then, you can simply combine all the ingredients, except the garnish, in a wide-mouth mug. (The shape of the mug is key, because the wider the top of the mug, the less you will smell the harsh, heated alcohol vapors as you drink and the more you will smell the flavors of the other ingredients.)

Or make the drink like the pros: Pour the warm water into the larger tin of a set of cocktail-shaking tins. Add the tea bag, if using, to infuse in the warm water. Now, nestle and float the smaller tin in the hot water. Use this small tin to begin mixing the drink. First, add the bourbon to warm it slowly, raising the temperature without muting flavors or diluting it. Next, add the syrup and a lemon slice to the warming bourbon. After 30 seconds or so, remove the floating tin from the tea water. Pour the hot tea water into the bourbon mixture, then pour it all in a wide-mouth mug. After infusing for 3 to 5 minutes, remove the tea bag.

GARNISHING TIP

Keep in mind that, because the water is warm, whatever garnish you add will infuse into the drink and add flavor. For this reason, do not garnish hot toddies with flowers, spices, or herbs unless they make sense and are intended to enhance the recipe. A cinnamon stick is a good choice if you are using other warm spice flavors in the syrup, such as chai, ginger, cinnamon, nutmeg, allspice, clove, or vanilla. Chamomile flowers are also very pretty floating in the mug. Citrus Wheels (page 138) are not meant to be eaten, but are a great option for adding texture and color to the glass.

MAKE IT NONALCOHOLIC: Leave out the spirit and add an ounce or two of cider or orange juice for a steaming, cozy mug of comfort. We like to make one and put it in a thermos for the cold, early mornings in the barn or watching our kids' sports.

SHOALWATER SEA BREEZE

Serves 1

1½ ounces vodka

3 ounces freshly squeezed pink grapefruit juice (about 1 grapefruit)

1 ounce Cranberry Rosemary Syrup (page 65)

Garnish: 1 rosemary sprig, about 6 inches tall, or Herb Bouquet (page 141)

9% ABV

244

We love this drink for a winter cocktail option that is fruity and sour, ideal for when we're feeling overwhelmed by the pumpkin, apple, and cinnamon flavors typical of winter drinks. Cranberry comes in, singing a whole other tune, possibly a New Wave hit. Cocktails have trends like anything else, but this update on the 1980s favorite, the Sea Breeze, has staying power.

For this comeback cocktail, we took the cranberry flavor and moved it from a cheap canned bar juice to a homemade syrup complemented by rosemary.

Use freshly squeezed grapefruit juice and you've taken a few delicious steps up in complexity from Venise's favorite classic cocktail, the Greyhound. It really makes a difference in this cocktail since it is the primary ingredient, and most bottled grapefruit juices have added sugar, which will make the drink overly sweet.

Shoalwater is the sea that surrounds the top coastal cranberry growing region in our home state of Washington, where we've taken our kids to the cranberry museum on stormy family beach trips before settling inside with a cocktail to watch the waves crash.

Fill an old-fashioned glass or 10-ounce juice cup with ice to the very top. Combine the vodka, grapefruit juice, and syrup in a cocktail shaker full of more ice. Shake for about 20 seconds, just until the outside of the shaker is cold. Strain the cocktail into your prepared glass to remove the juice pulp. Strip the bottom few inches of leaves off the rosemary sprig before adding it to the glass.

HEART BEET

Serves 1

1 fresh orange wheel

½ ounce rosemary simple syrup
(see Note)

½ ounce Beet Shrub (page 77)

1 ounce New American gin, such as
The Botanist

¼ ounce Cointreau or triple sec

2 ounces prosecco

Garnish: rosemary sprig,
just 1 to 2 inches long

14% ABV

Showing off the versatility of something as pointedly specific as a Beet Shrub (page 77), this cocktail couldn't be more different than the Bull's Blood & Bourbon recipe (page 247): a tall glass in place of short, herbaceous instead of earthy, refreshing and light where the other is intense. If you have Cointreau, a brand of orange liqueur, use it. If you don't, a generic triple sec works fine. A prosecco finish brings flavor and sweetness to the cocktail, but you could use club soda in a pinch to top it off. We understand that a drink with two liquors is already a lot to ask. We wouldn't have included it if it wasn't worth the effort, though!

Muddle the orange wheel at the bottom of your cocktail shaker, then add the syrup, beet shrub, gin, and triple sec. Shake for 20 seconds and strain into a wineglass. Top with chilled prosecco and garnish with a tiny rosemary sprig laid in the glass.

NOTE: For rosemary simple syrup, follow the Cranberry Rosemary Syrup instructions (page 65), but replace the cranberry juice with water.

FIGGY PUDDING FIZZ

Serves 1

½ ounce Orchardist Liqueur
(page 107)

1½ ounces Brown Butter Vodka
(page 107)

1 ounce Fig Cardamom Shrub
(page 80)

3 ounces club soda

Garnish: dried fig or a
cinnamon stick

10.5% ABV

Sometimes, the name comes first and we create around it, as was the case with this cocktail. "Pudding" is in the name for obvious Christmassy reasons, and the drink is on the sweet side, but it stays balanced due to the acidity of the vinegar-based shrub. The brown butter wash of the vodka brings a rich silkiness. Fig is an unsung holiday flavor that deserves a place on your menu beyond being wrapped in bacon or spread on toasts.

Combine the liqueur, vodka, and shrub in a cocktail shaker and shake for 15 seconds. Strain the cocktail into a tall glass filled with ice and top with the club soda. Garnish with a fig speared with a toothpick or a cinnamon stick.

BULL'S BLOOD & BOURBON

Serves 1

1½ ounces bourbon

2 ounces Beet Shrub (page 77)

½ ounce freshly squeezed
lemon juice

1 ounce club soda

2-inch ice cube or sphere

Garnish: pickled beet cube

11% ABV

If you've made the beet shrub already, willingly, you may not need convincing, but maybe you've flipped to the back of the book and found this drink and need to be convinced on why someone would combine anything with bourbon, an oft-served-neat spirit sacred in its lack of adornment, let alone beets. So, here is our speech to you: Beets are chock-full of natural sugar, and there is an earthiness to the root vegetable that is lovely when combined with the toasty, caramelized sugar flavors of bourbon. Imagine sprinkling brown sugar over a sheet pan of roasted carrots and parsnips, and then letting them roast until the edges begin to brown and all the flavors intensify. It's sort of like that, and you will see for yourself when you make it.

We like to grow deep red beets like this cocktail's namesake, the Bull's Blood Beet, which is preferred for its sweetness and lack of a bitter after-taste, as well as the short 55 days from planting to harvest growing time.

Don't use your best bourbon, by any means—always make cocktails with something not too precious. Be sure to shake the drink long enough to be very cold and dilute the shrub, or the acidity from the vinegar will be bracing and make your throat tickle.

Combine the bourbon, shrub, and lemon juice in a cocktail shaker, along with a cup of ice. Shake for 20 seconds, then strain the cocktail into a chilled old-fashioned glass with a 2-inch ice cube or sphere. Spear a pickled beet cube on a long bar toothpick and rest this across the top of the glass.

247

"IT WAS MUTUAL" HIGHBALL

Serves 1

1½ ounces aged rum or bourbon

½ ounce Scotch

2 dashes Barkeep's Citrus Bitters
(page 89)

½ ounce Fig Cardamom Shrub
(page 80)

3 ounces club soda

Garnish: fresh fig (if available)
and 1 sprig thyme

14% ABV

Figs are a wild and tasty example of nature's complexity and inter-dependence. "Mutualism" is the biological term for a relationship between two species that benefits them both. This cocktail gets its name from the intense relationship between wasps and figs. Commercially grown figs have been cultivated to not depend on pollination, but most fig trees do. Although generally considered a fruit, figs are technically an inverted flower. All flowers require pollination to bloom, and to pollinate a fig, the pollinator must crawl inside the inverted flower. There, female wasps pollinate the fig. Afterward, the figs ripen into delicious fruit, while the wasps die inside before they are quickly broken down by an enzyme called ficin and absorbed by the plant. Wild, right?

Build the drink directly in an empty, chilled collins glass: Add the rum or bourbon, Scotch, bitters, and shrub. Add ice to fill the glass. Top with the club soda. Stir once with a barspoon. Garnish with a fresh fig, if available, and a thyme sprig.

NOTE: The Scotch inclusion is important to impart the smoky peatiness, so don't skip it. Do not use the best, most precious aged Scotch in the house. A midshelf option, such as Dewar's, is a great option for cocktails that is affordable and widely available.

248

ACKNOWLEDGMENTS

To the moms—Denise, Melinda, Jill, and Debi—for your examples, encouragement, and babysitting. We raise a glass in thanks to our extended families, for the stories and food memories in these chapters, all filled with love. To our husbands—Troy and Ross—and to our kids—Henry, Hayes, Deyton, and Cash—for their patience while we worked on this book for a full year of our lives, and for their participation in every part of our business, including their hand modeling and taste testing for this book.

To Jill, our stepmom, who owned a health food store in New York City decades before organic was cool and taught us so much about growing and enjoying real food, and who supported Belinda's earliest floral concoctions business (a perfumery at the end of the driveway for which she donated recycled glass bottles and gave us the run of her garden). To our Dad, Uncle Darryl, Aunt Sheri, and Grandpa Val for the hours behind the counter at the Millwork Outlet, teaching us what a family business could look like. To Aunt Sylvia and Uncle Denis, for so many garden tours and every recipe or basket of berries you've sent home with us—the little things mean a lot. To Mom, for instilling in us an early love of books, healthy appetites, and for showing us how impactful a good

nonalcoholic option can be at a party—and in a person's life.

To Ina, Martha, Alice, Samin, Allison, Renee, Heather, and all of the other women in food who have served as mentors through their writing and recipes, thank you for cooking, and thank you for sharing. Anyone can cook, what matters is the sharing of the food.

To Sage, for her brilliant designs that have shaped this book's cover, and really our entire company, and Karna for your editing and taste testing (the tootsie roll realization.) To our mentor, Mary Heffernan (@FiveMarys), thank you for sharing your expertise and your literary agent, and hopping on a few frantic phone calls during the wild process that is first-time authorship. To Meg, for assisting during photoshoots and in life, and keeping the shop ship-shape.

Thank you to our agent, Leslie, for believing in this book from the first phone call and finding its home at Countryman Press. To our editor, Ann, thank you for the tough love to make this book the best it can be.

And thank you to Rylea, whose photographs always bring our vision to life and whose stories kept even the most intense shoot days light and fun. Your talent behind the camera brought us together, but your friendship was essential in crafting this book. And you look great in red lipstick.

INDEX

A

Among the Wildflowers, 208
Apple Betty Martini, 229
apple brandy, in Bonfire, 229
Apple Butter, 66
Apple Cider, Fresh-Pressed, 114
Asparagus, Quick-Pickled, 152
At High Noon, 171

B

Back Porch Lemonade, 219
Bailey's Irish Cream, in Plenty Good, 236
Barkeep's Citrus Bitters, 89
basil, 40
  Lime Basil Syrup, 54
beer
  Among the Wildflowers, 208
  Cock's Crow, 228
  Making Hay Shandy, 187
  Michelada, 224
Bee's Knees, 192

beet
  Heart Beet, 245
  Shrub, 77
berry(ies). *See also* blackberry;
    marionberry(ies);
    strawberry(ies)
  in Creamy Tea Cobbler, 173
  Liqueur, 105
  Rum, 105
  in Smash, 215
Bitters
  Barkeep's Citrus, 89
  & Soda, 166
Blackberry and Mint Syrup, 51. *See
    also* marionberry(ies)
Bloody Bunny, 201
Bloody Mary, 222
  Mix, 222
Bloody Mary Skewers, 140
Bonfire, 229
botanical gin drinks
  Bloody Bunny, 201
  Buzz Button Gin, 92

Clarified Milk Punch, 197
Elderflower Spritz, 203
Elderflower Vesper, 206
Lilac and Lead French 75, 185
Seattle Sling, 227
Southside, 213
Botanical Waters, 119
bourbon drinks
  Apple Betty Martini, 229
  Buck, 183
  Bull's Blood &, 247
  Home for the Holidays on the
    Ranch, 235
  Hot Toddy, 242
  "It Was Mutual" Highball, 248
  Old-Fashioned, 188
  Walk in the Woods, 209
brandy. *See* apple brandy
Brown Butter Vodka, 107
Buck, 183
  Nonalcoholic, 167
Bull's Blood & Bourbon, 247
Buzz Button Gin, 92

C

canning, 29

Cardamom Shrub, Fig, 80

carrots

  in Bloody Bunny, 201

  Pickled, 153

celery

  Pickled, 157

  Shrub, 74

chamomile, 35

  Lemon Chamomile Shrub, 73

Champagne

  Green Goddess, 206

  Lilac And Lead French 75, 185

cheese, in Bloody Mary Skewers, 140

Cherry Whiskey and Whiskey-Soaked

    Cherries, 95

chile peppers

  Pepper Hot Sauce, 81

  Pepper Tincture, 87

  Poblano Liqueur, 99

  Strawberry, Pepper and Mint

    Shrub, 71

chive

  Blossoms, Pickled, 158

  Flower Braids, 139

cider

  Fresh-Pressed Apple, 114

  Hot Spiced, 175

citrus. See also grapefruit; lemon;

    lemonade; lime; orange

  Barkeep's Citrus Bitters, 89

  Cordial, 59

  in Oleo Saccharum with Herbs, 58

  Peels, Candied, 136

  Wheels, 138

classic Coke, in Midnight at the

    Movies, 215

Classic Egg Cream, 174

Coastal Collins, 198

Cobbler, Creamy Tea, 173

Cock's Crow, 228

cocktail gardening, 32–43

  edible flowers, 35, 36–37

  essential plants, 35, 40–41

  planning the garden, 42–43

  pruning and harvesting, 41–42

cocktails, 178–248

  Among the Wildflowers, 208

  Apple Betty Martini, 229

  Back Porch Lemonade, 219

  Bee's Knees, 192

  Bloody Bunny, 201

  Bloody Mary, 222

  Bloody Mary Mix, 222

  Bonfire, 229

  Buck, 183

  Bull's Blood & Bourbon, 247

  Clarified Milk Punch, 197

  Coastal Collins, 198

  Cock's Crow, 228

  Crown Jewel, 205

  Cucumber Basil Gimlet, 216

  The Dashing Gentleman, 218

  Elderflower Spritz, 203

  Elderflower Vesper, 206

  Figgy Pudding Fizz, 245

  Garden Gibson, 202

  Garden Party Pitcher, 203

  Green Goddess, 206

  Hard Seltzer or Ranch Water, 181

  Harvest Moon Punch, 240

  Heart Beet, 245

  Homecoming Margarita, 231

  Home for the Holidays on the

    Ranch, 235

  Hot Toddy, 242

  "It Was Mutual" Highball, 248

  Lilac and Lead French 75, 185

Making Hay Shandy, 187

Margarita, 190

Marionberry Mojito, 210

Michelada, 224

Midnight at the Movies, 215

Nancy's Whiskey Sour, 232

Old-Fashioned, 188

Pitcher Margarita, 191

Pitcher Punch, 221

Pitcher Sangria, 194

Plenty Good, 236

Pumpkin Spice Espresso Martini, 237

Red Skies at Night, 184

Roman's Empire, 192

Seattle Sling, 227

Shoalwater Sea Breeze, 244

Smash, 215

Southside, 213

Sparkler, 239

Sparkling Rosé Wine Spritzer, 182

Spruce Drop, 204

Verde Maria, 224

Walk in the Woods, 209

White Sangria, 194

coffee

  Iced, 176

  Pumpkin Spice Espresso Martini, 237

Cointreau drinks

  Heart Beet, 245

  Homecoming Margarita, 231

  Margarita, 190

  Pitcher Margarita, 191

Compound Gin, 90

Cordial Spritz, 169. See also syrups

    and cordials

Cranberry Rosemary Syrup, 65

Crown Jewel, 205

Cucamelons, Pickled, 155

cucumber(s)

  Basil Gimlet, 216

Garlic Dill, Quick-Pickled, 156
   in Green Juice, 116
   Veggie Garden Vodka, 100

D

The Dashing Gentleman, 218
dehydrating. *See* juices, teas, and
      dehydrating
Dirty Soda, 174
drink crafting techniques, 26–29
Drink Your Garden tips, 21

E

edible flower(s), 35
   in Botanical Waters, 119
   Floral Salt or Sugar, 148
   guide to, 36–37
Egg Cream, Classic, 174
elderberries, in Onyx Oxymel, or
      Honey Shrub, 78
elderflower, 40
   Cordial, Foraged, 61
   Garden Party Pitcher, 203
   (or Lilac) Liqueur, 106
   Spritz, 203
   Vesper, 206
equipment and pantry list, 22–24
Espresso Martini, Pumpkin Spice, 237

F

fennel, 41
   Pollen Salt, 148
Fennelcello, 109
Fig Cardamom Shrub, 80
Figgy Pudding Fizz, 245
Fir or Spruce Tips, 40. *See also* Spruce
      (or Fir) Tip Syrup

Floral Salt or Sugar, 148
Floral Tea Blend (Non-Caffeinated), 125
Floral Water, Distilled, 127
flowers and herbs. *See also* edible
      flower(s); *specific types*
   Drying For Tea, 122
   Hang-Drying, 120
French 75, Lilac and Lead, 185
fruit. *See also specific fruits and berries*
   Stone Fruit Tea, 126

G

Garden Gibson, 202
gardening. *See* cocktail gardening
Garden Party Pitcher, 203
garlic
   Dill Cucumbers, Quick-Pickled,
      156
   Scapes, Asparagus, Or Green Beans,
      Quick-Pickled, 152
garnishes, 130–49. *See also* refrigerator
      pickles, quick; rimming salts
      and sugars
   Bloody Mary Skewers, 140
   Candied Citrus Peels, 136
   Chive Flower Braids, 139
   Citrus Wheels, 138
   Fancy Ice, 135
   Herb Bouquets, 141
   Mojito Berries, 144
Gibson, Garden, 202
Gimlet, Cucumber Basil, 216
gin
   Buzz Button, 92
   Compound, 90
gin drinks
   Back Porch Lemonade, 219
   Bloody Bunny, 201
   Buck, 183

Crown Jewel, 205
Cucumber Basil Gimlet, 216
Elderflower Spritz, 203
Garden Gibson, 202
Harvest Moon Punch, 240
Heart Beet, 245
Southside, 213
Ginger Switchel, 75
grapefruit
   Roman's Empire, 192
   Shoalwater Sea Breeze, 244
Green Beans, Quick-Pickled, 152
Green Goddess, 206
Green Juice, 116
greens
   in Green Juice, 116
   Kale and Chard Vodka, 101

H

Hard Seltzer or Ranch Water, 181
Harvesting and Pruning, 41–42
Harvest Moon Punch, 240
Heart Beet, 245
herb(s). *See also specific herbs*
   in Botanical Waters, 119
   Bouquets, 141
   and Flowers, Drying for Tea, 122
   and Flowers, Hang-Drying, 120
   Garden Salt, Spicy, 147
   harvesting, 42
   Oleo Saccharum with, 58
   and plants, essential, 35, 40–41
   Sugar, 149
   in Sun Tea, 126
   Tincture, 86
Highball, "It Was Mutual," 248
Homecoming Margarita, 231
Home for the Holidays on the Ranch
      (to Find Love), 235

253

honey
    Lavender Honey Syrup, 57
    Shrub, 78
Hot Spiced Cider, 175
Hot Toddy, 242

I

Ice, Fancy, 135
Iced Coffee, 176
Iced Tea, 170
infused spirits. *See* tinctures,
        liqueurs, and infused spirits
infusions, 29, 30–31
ingredients, stocking, 24–25
"It Was Mutual" Highball, 248

J

Jalapeño Tequila, 96
Juices, Teas, and Dehydrating, 110–28
    Botanical Waters, 119
    Distilled Floral Water, 127
    Drying Flowers and Herbs for Tea,
        122
    Floral Tea Blend (Non-
        Caffeinated), 125
    Fresh-Pressed Apple Cider, 114
    Fresh Tomato Juice, 117
    Green Juice, 116
    Hang-Drying Flowers and Herbs,
        120–21
    Juicing for Cocktail Recipes, 113
    Stone Fruit Tea, 126
    Sun Tea, 126
juniper berries, in Compound Gin,
    90

K

Kale and Chard Vodka, 101

L

Lavender, 40
    Honey Syrup, 57
lemon
    balm/mint, 35
    Chamomile Shrub, 73
    Citrus Wheels, 138
    in Pitcher Punch, 221
Lemonade by the Pitcher, Fresh, 168
lilac, 40–41
    Cordial, 60
    and Lead French 75, 185
    Liqueur, 106
lime
    Basil Syrup, 54
    Shrub, Spiced, No-Waste, 75
liqueur. *See also* Cointreau;
        Maraschino liqueur
    Basic, 85
    Berry, 105
    Elderflower (or Lilac), 106
    Orchardist, 107
    Poblano, 99
liquor cabinet, stocking, 26

M

Maraschino liqueur, in the Dashing
        Gentleman, 218
Margarita, 190
    Homecoming, 231
    Pitcher, 191
marionberry(ies)
    in Blackberry and Mint Syrup, 51
    Mojito, 210
martini(s). *See also* Elderflower Vesper
    Apple Betty, 229
    Garden Gibson, 202
    Pumpkin Spice Espresso, 237
mezcal, in Homecoming Margarita, 231
Michelada, 224

Midnight at the Movies, 215
Milk Punch, Clarified, 197
mint, 35
    Blackberry and Mint Syrup, 51
    Strawberry, Pepper and Mint
        Shrub, 71
    in Sun Tea, 126
mocktails. *See* nonalcoholic drinks
Mojito, Marionberry, 210
Mojito Berries, 144

N

nectarines, in Stone Fruit Tea, 126
nonalcoholic drinks, 160–76
    Bitters & Soda, 166
    Cordial Spritz, 169
    Creamy Tea Cobbler, 173
    Dirty Soda and the Classic Egg
        Cream, 174
    Fresh Lemonade by the Pitcher, 168
    At High Noon, 171
    Hot Spiced Cider, 175
    Iced Coffee, 176
    Iced Tea, 170
    Nonalcoholic Buck, 167
    Shrub Soda, 164
    Simple Syrup Soda, 164
    Strawberries and Cream Soda, 163

O

Old-Fashioned, 188
Oleo Saccharum with Herbs, 58
Onyx Oxymel, or Honey Shrub, 78
orange
    Candied Citrus Peels, 136
    Citrus Wheels, 138
    in Sangria, 194
orange liqueur. *See* Cointreau
Orchardist Liqueur, 107

254

P

pantry and equipment list, 22–24
peaches, in Stone Fruit Tea, 126
pears, in Orchardist Liqueur, 107
Pepper Hot Sauce, 81
Pepper Tincture, 87
Pitcher Margarita, 191
Pitcher Punch, 221
Pitcher Sangria, 194
Plenty Good, 236
plums, in Stone Fruit Tea, 126
Poblano Liqueur, 99
Prosecco, in Heart Beet, 245
Pruning and Harvesting, 41–42
pumpkin
    Spice Espresso Martini, 237
    Spice Syrup, 62
punch
    Clarified Milk, 197
    Harvest Moon, 240
    Pitcher, 221

R

Ranch Water, 181
Red Skies at Night, 184
Refrigerator Pickles, Quick, 150–58
    Garlic Dill Cucumbers, Quick-
        Pickled, 156
    Garlic Scapes, Asparagus, or Green
        Beans, Quick-Pickled, 152
    Pickled Carrots, 153
    Pickled Celery, 157
    Pickled Chive Blossoms, 158
    Pickled Cucamelons, 155
rimming salts and sugars, 146–49
    Fennel Pollen Salt, 148
    Floral Salt or Sugar, 148
    Herb Sugar, 149
    Spicy Herb Garden Salt, 147
    Vanilla Sugar, 149

Roman's Empire, 192
rosemary, 41
    Cranberry Rosemary Syrup, 65
rose petals, in distilled floral water, 127
Rosé Wine Spritzer, Sparkling, 182
rum
    Berry Rum, 105
    in Mojito Berries, 144
    in Tinctures, 86, 87
rum drinks
    Buck, 183
    "It Was Mutual" Highball, 248
    Marionberry Mojito, 210
    Red Skies at Night, 184
rye whiskey drinks
    Nancy's Whiskey Sour, 232
    Old-Fashioned, 188
    Smash, 215

S

salami, in Bloody Mary Skewers, 140
salt. *See* rimming salts and sugars
Sangria, 194
Scotch drinks
    Bonfire, 229
    "It Was Mutual" Highball, 248
Seattle Sling, 227
Shandy, Making Hay, 187
Shoalwater Sea Breeze, 244
Shrub(s), 68–81
    Basic, 70
    Beet, 77
    Celery, 74
    Fig Cardamom, 80
    Lemon Chamomile, 73
    No-Waste Spiced Lime, aka Ginger
        Switchel, 75
    Onyx Oxymel, or Honey, 78
    Pepper Hot Sauce, 81
    Strawberry, Pepper and Mint, 71

Shrub Soda, 164
Simple Syrup
    Basic Flavored, 48
    Soda, 164
Smash, 215
soda(s)
    Bitters &, 166
    Dirty, 174
    Shrub, 164
    Simple Syrup, 164
    Strawberries and Cream, 163
Southside, 213
Sparkler, 239
sparkling wine drinks. *See also*
        Champagne; Prosecco
    Green Goddess, 206
    Harvest Moon Punch, 240
    Sparkler, 239
    Sparkling Rosé Wine Spritzer, 182
Spritz, Elderflower, 203
Spruce Drop, 204
spruce or fir tips, 40
Spruce (or Fir) Tip Syrup, 53
Stone Fruit Tea, 126
strawberry(ies)
    and Cream Soda, 163
    Strawberry, Pepper, and Mint
        Shrub, 71
    Syrup, 50
sugar. *See* rimming salts and sugars
Sun Tea, 126
Swiss chard, in Kale and Chard
        Vodka, 101
Syrups and Cordials, 46–67
    Apple Butter, 66
    Basic Flavored Simple Syrup, 48
    Blackberry and Mint Syrup, 51
    Citrus Cordial, 59
    Cranberry Rosemary Syrup, 65
    Foraged Elderflower Cordial, 61
    Lavender Honey Syrup, 57

255

Syrups and Cordials (*continued*)
  Lilac Cordial, 60
  Lime Basil Syrup, 54
  Oleo Saccharum with Herbs, 58
  Pumpkin Spice Syrup, 62
  Spruce (or Fir) Tip Syrup, 53
  Strawberry Syrup, 50

T

tea
  Blend (Non-Caffeinated), Floral,
    125
  Creamy Tea Cobbler, 173
  Drying Flowers and Herbs for, 122
  Iced, 170
  in Milk Punch, Clarified, 197
  Stone Fruit, 126
  Sun, 126
techniques. *See* drink crafting
    techniques
Tequila, Jalapeño, 96
tequila drinks. *See also* mezcal
  Buck, 183
  Cock's Crow, 228
  Hard Seltzer or Ranch Water, 181
  Homecoming Margarita, 231
  Pitcher Margarita, 191
  Poblano Liqueur, 99
  Verde Maria, 224
Tinctures, Liqueurs, and Infused
    Spirits, 82–109
  Barkeep's Citrus Bitters, 89
  Basic Liqueur, 85

Berry Rum and Berry Liqueur, 105
Brown Butter Vodka, 107
Buzz Button Gin, 92
Cherry Whiskey and Whiskey-
  Soaked Cherries, 95
Compound Gin, 90
Elderflower (or Lilac) Liqueur, 106
Fennelcello, 109
Herb Tincture, 86
Jalapeño Tequila, 96
Kale and Chard Vodka, 101
Orchardist Liqueur, 107
Pepper Tincture, 87
Poblano Liqueur, 99
Veggie Garden Vodka, 100
tomatillos
  Veggie Garden Vodka, 100
  in Verde Maria, 224
tomato(es)
  in Bloody Mary Mix, 222
  Juice, Fresh, 117
toothache plant, 41. *See also* Buzz
    Button Gin

V

Vanilla Sugar, 149
Veggie Garden Vodka, 100
Verde Maria, 224
vermouth drinks
  Dashing Gentleman, 218
  Seattle Sling, 227
Vesper, Elderflower, 206
Viognier, in Sangria, 194

vodka
  Brown Butter, 107
  Kale and Chard, 101
  Veggie Garden, 100
vodka drinks
  Back Porch Lemonade, 219
  Berry Rum, 105
  Buck, 183
  Coastal Collins, 198
  Compound Gin, 90
  Distilled Floral Water, 127
  Elderflower Vesper, 208
  Fennelcello, 109
  Orchardist Liqueur, 107
  Pumpkin Spice Espresso Martini,
    237
  Roman's Empire, 192
  Shoalwater Sea Breeze, 244
  Spruce Drop, 204

W

Walk in the Woods, 209
wheat whiskey drinks
  Among the Wildflowers, 208
Whiskey, Cherry, 95
whiskey drinks. *See* bourbon; rye
    whiskey; Scotch; wheat whiskey
Whiskey-Soaked Cherries, 95
White Sangria, 194
wine. *See also* Champagne; sparkling
    wine; vermouth; Viognier
  red, in Bonfire, 229
  Spritzer, Sparkling Rosé, 182

256